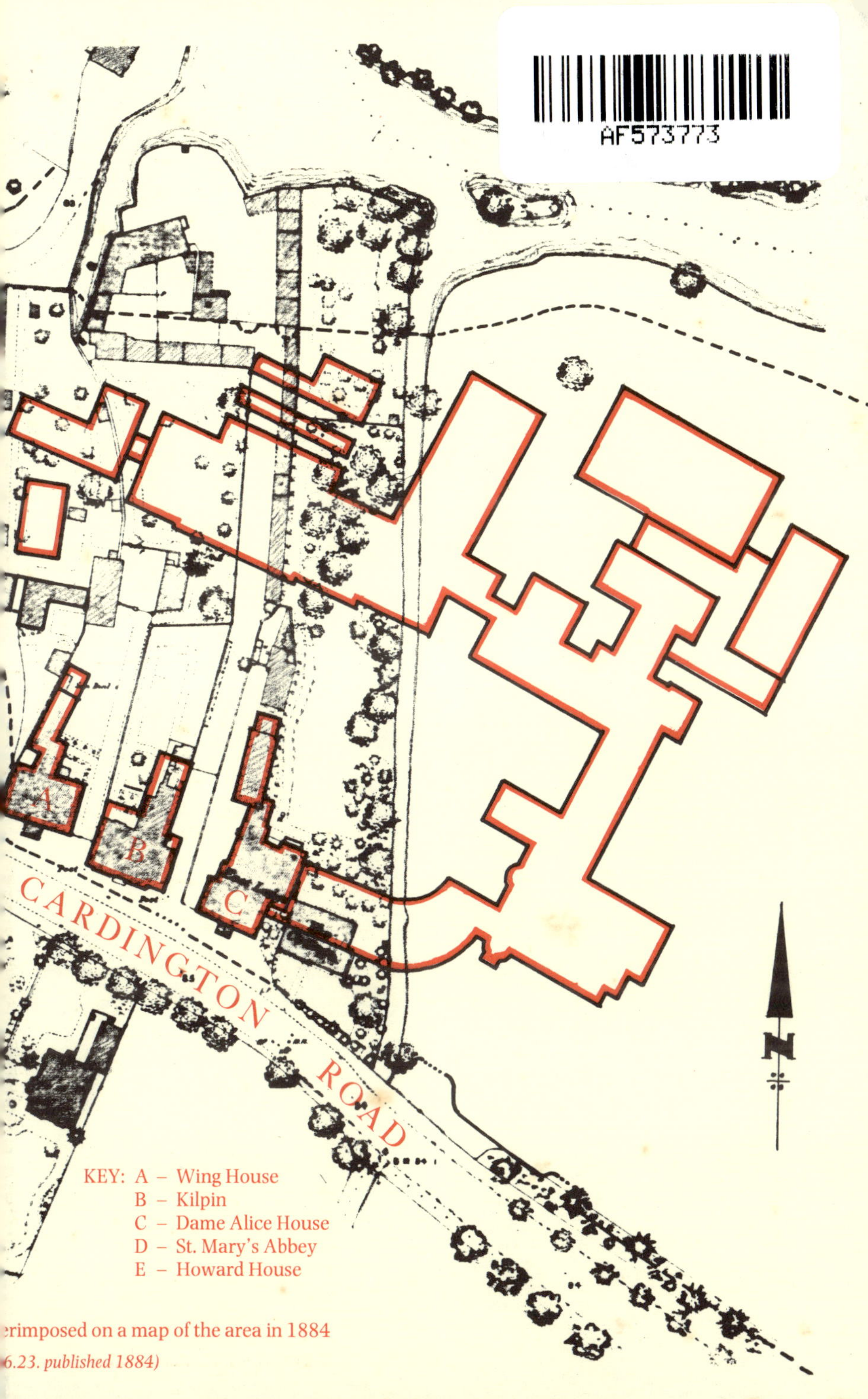

erimposed on a map of the area in 1884

6.23. published 1884)

The History of the School

The History of the School

Constance M. Broadway & Esther I. Buss

1882 B.G.M.S.–D.A.H.S. 1982

ISBN 0 950806 00 5

1st Edition 1982
Printed by White Crescent Press Ltd, Luton, England

Foreword

A Centenary is a good time to take stock, a time to look back as well as forward. How often do we become so engrossed in the worries of modern life that we tend to overlook those of the past? Most of the time, I suspect. How often do we pause to think that we are making history? Seldom, if ever. A Centenary puts the present into perspective and makes one aware of more than the immediate future.

The life of Bedford Girls' Modern School has never been an easy one. Successive headmistresses have fought for its existence, schemed and planned its future in a way that makes our own struggle for independence, high standards and even survival seem less daunting.

I am indebted to my three colleagues who have worked so hard to produce this book. Constance Broadway's death occurred before she could finish the text and saddened us all. She was Head of the History Department from 1948 until her retirement in 1975. It was right that this task should have been completed by her former pupil Esther Buss (*née* Kingham). Esther Buss also taught History at Dame Alice. The cover has been designed by Barbara Wells, also an Old Girl, and later Head of the Art Department from 1946 to 1973.

But, as the title suggests, there is not only history in this book, there is a school and a school is people. This book is full of people; I hope you will enjoy meeting them or renewing their acquaintance.

S. M. MORSE

Acknowledgements

Thanks are due to the following:

All those who helped in the collection of material:

The Headmistress and staff of The Dame Alice Harpur School, those in the County Record Office, R. N. Hutchins and the staff of the Harpur Trust.

Mary Wilkinson for gathering material from Old Girls – and all those who sent in their 'memories'.

Miss Elizabeth Gilroy for her help.

Ann Davies for her sketches.

Mrs Felicity Hunter who contributed further information on Miss Porter, the first Head Mistress.

All those who have helped in the actual preparation of the script – those who typed, checked and prepared the charts.

All those whose encouragement helped throughout.

Contents

1882
May 1.

The Girls Modern School
Bedford

This School was opened on May 1st for work with 58 pupils present the number being increased in a fortnight to 73 in attendance

Mary E. Porter.

Bromham Road to St. Paul's Square 1882–1894

The first term

The first page of the first log book, written in Miss Porter's strong angular hand, starts thus:

1882 May 1. This school was opened on May 1st for *work* with *58 pupils* present, the number being increased in a fortnight to 73 in attendance.

The 58 pupils, from little Nellie Roff, the youngest, aged 7, to the 'big' girls, Annie Thomlinson and Augusta Biggs (aged 15) started the term by listening to Psalm 67 'God be merciful unto us and bless us'. Miss Porter then addressed them in serious terms, exhorting them 'as foundation stones' of the new school to make good use of their 'many privileges and advantages' so that in time to come they might look back on their past school life and 'not only feel proud of your school, of the creditable work which you and others have done here, but that you should be able to feel that God blessed you here, gave you more earnest thoughts about your life and its duties, and a great desire to be helpful to others.' So, after a prayer, they started work.

The girls were quickly divided into four forms, the little ones under Mrs Southgate in Form I, while Miss March, Miss Gillie and Miss Cooper took the three other groups. From the beginning French and German and Class Singing were the responsibility of part-time specialists.

Their presence in the new Jacobean-styled building in Bromham Road that May Day morning was the result of a long series of events which had started before they were born.

The growing interest in and need for mass elementary education had led in 1815 to the establishment of the Harpur 'National' or Monitorial School, but the move to use its premises for the education of girls on Tuesday and Thursday afternoons was not popular, and pupils were few. The project was discontinued and it was not till 1836 – the year before Queen Victoria ascended the throne – that a viable girls' elementary school was started. So in 1873 when the new scheme for the Harpur Trust was given Royal Assent, there was available some experience of the needs of girls' education. A Special Committee was founded to prepare for the creation of the two girls' schools, and, to the dismay of some members of the Trust, five women were co-opted on to it. They included Miss Mary Ewart, a benefactor of Newnham College, Cambridge, and Miss Smith from the University Museum, Oxford. At last, girls were to have an 'integral but inferior' share in the endowment; 4/11ths of the annual income was to be given to the Boys' Modern School and its sister establishment, but for the purposes of the grant, five girls were to count as three boys (as indeed they did until 1969). It was necessary to accumulate funds before building could start and during the waiting period the Governors temporarily lost heart and decided to build only the Girls' Modern School. Social pride and local determination led to a petition which reversed this plan and a building was designed by Basil Champneys for the site of the old, redundant almshouses, which should provide for 200 pupils at the Girls' Modern and 100 at the High School.

The new buildings, still the central part of the High School erected by S. Foster of Kempston at an initial cost of about £11,000, featured a central Hall, to be shared by the two schools, and capable of being partitioned by sliding doors. The elegance of the Hall, with its high dado and graceful, festooned frieze and the efficiency of its up-to-date gas lighting and patent ventilation system, were much admired. On either side, the schools had their independent premises – the High School a little more ornate both outside and in than the Modern School. In front, the trees already on the site were retained, and behind the High School section a Gymnasium and a Cookery room were provided.

The first term's work proceeded quietly; a visit from three Governors on 18th May led to an expression of approval for the First Form's Arithmetic lesson, but the climax came on 20th July with the official opening of the schools by Lady Isabella Whitbread.

The carriages of the guests passed under a triumphal arch which was erected from the corner of Adelaide Square to Gwyn Street; Venetian masts decked the outside of the school; St. Paul's bells rang and the Promenade Band played in the playground. Inside the Hall an orchestra and the vocalists of the Musical Society were ready to entertain. The pupils, their parents and an invited audience were faced by a dignified platform party including the Lord Lieutenant The Right Hon. Earl Cowper K.G., four M.P.s, the Mayor, the Governors, Aldermen, Councillors and members of the Trust.

May Billson for the High School, and Nellie Roff, the youngest of the Modern School pupils, made their way from the back of the Hall to present roses and a card, lettered with the inscription recording the day's events, to Lady Isabella. They were lifted up for a kiss before rejoining their friends. Then the speeches began – Lord Cowper's, general and rather condescending, Dr Storrar's, informative and hopeful, defining clearly the position of the Modern School. 'In that school the education begins at 7 and may continue to the age of 17, but exhibitions will be granted to carry promising pupils into the High School, to continue their education there until the age of 19 or 20.' Mr Whitbread spoke movingly about the schools – 'They start with a share of a great endowment, and in all human probability they will continue. . . . They start with another great advantage. They are not tied down to any class, they are not fettered by any creed or formulary at all; they are perfectly open, I may say, to the whole world.'

So the great day ended with singing, and the schools returned to their work, and to the building of that *esprit de corps* which had become so much a feature of boys' public school education. And the first term was over.

Miss Porter

Not a great deal is known about Miss Porter's earlier career. She was apparently a north country woman, born in 1836, educated at Queen's College, London, and by 1860 the headmistress of the school owned by a Miss Heathcoat at Bolham, near Tiverton, for the training of the daughters of professional men as private governesses. Here there were 40 pupils, plus a small class of little children aged from 7–10 or 12, who were taught by the young ladies. She herself was in charge of religious teaching, and is later referred to by an ex-pupil as being English mistress there, perhaps before she became headmistress.

While giving evidence before the Schools' Inquiry Commission in March 1866, she intimated that she was about to open a private school of her own in the north at Gateshead, for day boarders, beginning with about thirty pupils. Nothing further is known at present about this venture, but in November 1871 she was appointed the first headmistress of Drake and Tonson's Girls' School, Keighley. She stayed there for a year only, but seems to have taken some pains to see it well-established before she left to become the very first G.P.D.S.T. headmistress at Chelsea (later Kensington High School) at the beginning of 1873.

Here there were many difficulties to contend with. The neighbourhood was unsuitable, the house was old and in need of constant repair: not only was she responsible for the teaching and organisation of the school, but also for the supervision of the domestic staff (with at first one full-time assistant and some part-time help); and shortage of funds was an ever-present problem. She stayed here only until January 1875, leaving to become the first headmistress of Bradford Grammar School for Girls which, as an endowed school, she felt would give her 'a greater sphere of usefulness'. Her testimonial from the Council commended her 'skill and earnestness in teaching'.

The centenary Chronicle of B.G.G.S. gives a brief outline of the early history of the school and contains the following information about Miss Porter. 'She was obviously dedicated to the cause of women's education and, though she looks formidable in her photograph, is described as a woman of rare tact and ability. She appears to have needed these qualities – the buildings were too small, badly ventilated and inconvenient, and the number of pupils had to be limited as the teaching power of four regular staff, with a mistress for French, and masters for drawing and class singing, could not undertake more than the original entry of 112 pupils. . . .

'Miss Porter's vocation was to found and establish good girls' schools and having achieved this at Bradford, she resigned in 1880. She had dealt firmly with many problems, including complaints, in letters to the *Bradford Observer*, about too much homework, too much teaching, and too restricted buildings. She had taken care to provide comfortable desks and to supervise herself the limited amount of physical exercise which could be provided in the cramped conditions.'

From Bradford, she appears to have gone to Castleton, as she is listed as 'Headmistress, Castleton', in the list of applicants for the post of headmistress in the Harpur Trust Minute Book.

Apart from her teaching and organising activities in school, while at Bolham she helped collect signatures for Emily Davies's successful campaign of 1864 to allow girls to be entered for the Cambridge Locals. She was also a member of the Kensington Society (a discussion society which covered topics such as women's education and suffrage and which lasted from 1865 for about three years). Among fellow-members were Emily Davies, Frances Buss, Dorothea Beale, Elizabeth Garrett (later Anderson), Millicent Garrett (later Fawcett), Sophia Jex-Blake, and Barbara Bodichon, to name but a few of the more famous.

While in the north she was secretary of the Newcastle and Gateshead Association of Schoolmistresses and was one of their two elected representatives on the North of England Council for the Promotion of Higher Education for Women.

She was a founder member of the Association of Headmistresses, being one of the nine at the first meeting in 1874. She hosted the annual conference at Bradford in March 1878 and thus became a Vice-President, while in 1879 she was elected to the first ever executive committee, but resigned two years later. She remained an active member while in Bedford, drafting the address presented to Queen Victoria on the occasion of her Jubilee in 1887, and in the same year attending the Uppingham Conference at which there were 57 present, including Miss Belcher from the High School.

Academic problems – staffing, curriculum, pupils

Her acceptance of the post at Bedford meant that again she faced many severe problems. It was difficult to find experienced and able staff and in the first years there were many changes. By July 1885 the four original full-time assistants had gone and by 1887 only Miss Lister and Miss Turner remained from the first year. The appointment in 1885 of Miss Alice Mary Smith was to give to the school one of its greatly loved and long serving teachers. Mary Smith had been educated at the French Protestant College, Bedford, and obtained a first class certificate at the Bedford Kindergarten Training College. She came straight from college to the school, where, for a starting salary of £40 a year, she taught History and English, Arithmetic, Needlework and Scripture. She stayed till her retirement in 1925.

Few women went to university, and a common way into the teaching profession was by becoming a pupil teacher and then gaining a place at one of the comparatively few teacher training colleges. This is illustrated by the career of Miss Boyd, who joined the staff in September 1882 as a student teacher, and in January 1883 was engaged as a form mistress for a term and remained until 1884, when Miss Porter records that she left 'as she was not a good disciplinarian'. Annie Thomlinson had a somewhat similar career. She entered the school on its first day, having been away from school a year, and on reaching the age of 17 she became a student teacher. By September 1884 she was being paid for her services and in 1885 she is listed with the form teachers, having charge of IIB, and in 1889 she took over IIA, remaining at the school until 1899.

To the girls, doubtless, they all seemed infinitely and equally old, and it was only years later that one pupil realised that the gold watch and chain and bangles which her teacher had displayed as birthday presents, actually marked her coming of age!

It was Miss Porter's consistent concern to establish and maintain a good academic standard, and she recorded with satisfaction the remarks of official visitors. Miss Smith (a Governor) liked Miss Cooper's History lesson very much in 1883 and a year later she was 'much pleased and thought a great advance had been made since she heard the teaching a year ago'. In February 1884 Miss Emily Davies (the Foundress of Girton) came and was so impressed that a plan was proposed for Girton students to come and observe.

At the end of the Summer term 1884 came the first of a series of examinations of the whole school. The report of the examination by Mr Belcher and Mr Tuckwell, who inspected both schools, throws some light on the work done. They deplored the lack of prizes as they felt that the girls were left motiveless, but Miss Porter disagreed with them. We learn that 'no girl in IVA seemed to understand the division of fractions', in V, 'three girls did excellent papers' in Botany and that IVA and IVB 'understood the process of fructification, fairly knew leaf structure and were familiar with the natural orders, but were less at home in the morphology'. Mr Belcher reported on Literature, History, French and Euclid. He wondered about the value of 'Outlines of Literature' for 'girls of larger growth' and made some useful suggestions for combining this work with History! IVA were in trouble again; their knowledge of their Shakespeare play was defective, but their parsing and analysis were good. French composition was 'uncommonly good', though only the V achieved a good clear style in translation.

A more formal approach to this annual inspection came in the following year, when the school was to be placed under the College of Preceptors for examination, an arrangement which was only interrupted by the move to St. Paul's Square in 1892 and continued till at least 1898. In 1886 the Senior School was examined by printed papers and the Juniors in a viva voce manner. The subjects were Reading, Writing, Dictation, Scripture, English Grammar, English Literature, History, Geography, Arithmetic and French. It seems that Outlines of English Literature still featured on the syllabus, but one wonders what the V form made of the literature period 449–1216! English History was the forte of IVA, while IVB did 'excellent work' in History and Scripture. In IIIB and the lower forms, Object Lessons were given, and it was suggested that the girls should be encouraged to write 'a brief sketch of the lesson, and be exercised in expressing in language exact, however simple, what is noted by them'. In IIB 'the copy books are neatly kept', but 'the English Grammar is a weak subject, many of the girls confounding nouns with verbs and having no clear notions at all of their functions'. Form I kept their copy books neatly and their answers in Scripture, Geography and History gave most distinct evidence of very careful, intelligent teaching.

Already the school was 'setted' for Arithmetic and for French. The examiners found the French good and even Form I had made an 'excellent beginning, the pronunciation being particularly good for such young children'. Botany and Euclid had temporarily been abandoned and the time used to improve other subjects. 'In every room,' said Mr Pincher, 'I saw good order, proper behaviour, cheerful obedience and honest willing work.'

This peep behind the scenes helps us to picture those girls of the Eighties, in their long frocks, frilly aprons, buttoned boots and black stockings, seated at their pitch pine desks, some at fixed double desks, others in lines at forms. They were often bitterly cold; Miss Porter told the Governors of the 'imperfect warming of the Great Hall and the larger classrooms'. She wrote, 'I have taught in one classroom where the thermometer was down to 38°F (only 6 degrees above freezing point) at my end of the room and I had to send the girls who sat at that end of the room to put on their outdoor clothes before I could give the lesson.' By the following year, it was warmer, but the problems of cold corridors and sickness remained.

During these early years, many girls who entered the school had been poorly taught and were considered 'backward', so every individual success was welcomed. The first 3 girls sent up to Junior Cambridge heard that they had all passed in March 1885, even though they all failed in Botany. In 1888 there were 5 candidates, 2 Senior and 3 Junior; in 1892 Miss Porter declared that in seven years, 26 girls had been entered for Cambridge Locals and 25 had passed. It was important to the school to advertise these successes. In the early years the Summer term ended with a Parents' Social, at which recitations and singing were a prelude to an address from Miss Porter. The general (and complimentary) remarks of the annual College of Preceptors' examiners were published in the *Bedfordshire Times*, as were the reports of the annual gathering of parents and pupils of 'Miss Porter's School' from 1890.

Leaving age

There were problems other than the academic ones. Miss Porter was in charge of a school which many of the Governors saw as definitely inferior to the High School, restricted as to the age of its pupils and intended to teach 'modern' subjects not the university orientated Classics. The strict imposition of the age limit of 17 years was soon to bring protests from Miss Porter, who was galled by seeing promising pupils leave or go on to the High School, when boys at the Modern School could readily obtain an exemption from the age limit.

On 1st May 1890, the Charity Commissioners refused to extend the age of attendance at B.G.M.S. to 18 years, though, as Miss Porter rather bitterly comments, they had not been asked for a general extension, only for special exemptions, recommended by the Headmistress and sanctioned by the Governors. After numbers had risen rapidly to 183 in 1884 there was a period of stagnation followed by a decline to 146 in 1894, and meanwhile the High School was forging ahead, with 553 girls in that year. It seemed as though parents who readily sent their sons to B.M.S. preferred their daughters to enjoy the social cachet and academic success of the High School.

Financial problems

With fees at £4 a year and a rent charge of £350 p.a. the school was almost immediately faced by financial problems. Before it was opened, the Governers had allotted £560 for the payment of assistants, and although in 1883 Miss Porter is writing in terms of £820 for teaching purposes, this is a reduction of £50 and in consequence German had to be removed from the curriculum and economies made in the cost of part-time singing teachers. A year later, the grant was down to £704 for staff and equipment and Miss Porter was driven to supplementing her official funds with £50 from her own income. She notes by way of contrast that the grant for the High School was £1,700. To deal with the situation, the two senior classes were combined, so saving the salary of a senior member of staff. In such circumstances, rumours circulated; it was said that girls were leaving to go to the High School because their parents were dissatisfied with the education given. The French teaching was singled out for criticism and the dropping of Botany from the curriculum led to adverse comment. In this sea of troubles, Miss Porter made valiant efforts to save the school. Faced with a debt from 1885–86 of £309, she offered to accept a reduction of salary. Her fixed salary was now to be £100 p.a. with capitation fees of £1 10s on the first 150 pupils (instead of £2) and 10s on the next 50 (instead of £1). This reduction, intended to be temporary, was continued till the end of the decade.

There was also, notably in 1890, some considerable anxiety among the Governors about the proportion of the 4/11ths of the charity which the girls were taking: 'there is every prospect that, in the near future, the share of the endowment will be materially diminished, for if the number in the Modern School for Girls increases, as there is every prospect of its doing, the income from the endowment will be proportionately reduced'. They therefore proposed an increase in the number of boarders allowed at the Boys' Modern School which among other things would serve to improve its financial position. A committee of Bedford householders prepared a Memorial for the Charity Commissioners opposing this, and urging instead a decrease in fees at B.M.S., and stating that in fact 'the Governors have discouraged the growth of the Modern School for Girls and have allowed a private arrangement in one of the elementary schools for girls whereby the growth of the Modern School for Girls is retarded (*Bedfordshire Times*, 8th November 1890).

Meanwhile, the outstanding success of the High School was causing pressure on the available space in the Bromham Road building. First a classroom was handed over, then the Hall itself, so that the Modern School used the Gymnasium for prayers and only the fortnightly moral lecture took place in the Hall. By 1887 the Governors were noting that it was desirable that the High School should acquire the whole of the buildings and that the Girls' Modern School should buy the Grammar School new building, about to fall vacant when the boys moved to their present site in St. Peter's Street. This move was to be financially advantageous for Miss Porter's school since the High School were to pay £9,400 for the Modern School's share of Bromham Road, but the cost of the Grammar School buildings was only £5,500. It must have been with great relief that Miss Porter saw the furniture and fittings of the Modern School installed in its new home, ceilings freshly white-washed, doors and dados painted and a covered way built to the Gymnasium. So a brass plate was fixed on the hand gate, fire regulations were discussed, and a new era began.

Pictures of Bromham Road

Miss Mary Smith, who taught for forty years at the school, has left us some vivid pictures of the years at Bromham Road. The highlight of the week was Miss Porter's address in the Hall. The Headmistress habitually wore a white mob cap, and as she 'finished with each sheet of her address, she just cast it away, and it floated slowly down on or near the platform, with many eyes fixed on it to see where it would settle. When she had finished she was surrounded by a flurry of white as if she had been out in a snow-storm.' Fridays, too, saw a weekly test with five questions in several subjects and one or two sums to do. In the afternoon all the school did Needlework. The girls brought from home any plain sewing their parents wished; some were most skilled, gathering and stroking and finely hemming shirt wrist bands. Others perhaps benefited from the special lessons in 'Scientific Cutting Out', available as an extra study. From 1888 these lessons led to the making of garments for Dr Barnardo's children, and this link with Dr Barnardo's Homes has remained throughout the history of the school.

Miss Porter was a cultured and well-travelled woman, something of an artist (she had exhibited at the Royal Academy) and for a time taught Drawing. She was not, however, a portraitist, and the pictures which she gave to decorate the blank walls at Bromham Road and St. Paul's Square were mainly woodland landscapes. Her other main contact with the girls came in her Scripture lessons. She always taught with the form mistress sitting in the room, correcting books. Perhaps it was this which helped to create a strained atmosphere in which wild answers led to children being sent to stand facing the wall. Miss Gillions, however, reports her enjoyment and lasting memories of Scripture lessons, and also the interesting term's lessons in elocution which Miss Porter gave.

At Bradford, in addition to teaching Scripture, Miss Porter had taught Swedish Drill. She appears to have retained her interest at Bedford, for Miss Smith tells how Miss Stansfeld came on Friday afternoons and gave lessons in it to both staff and Headmistress, which they passed on to the children later on. 'I remember how taken aback I was to find myself the partner of the Headmistress in one of those queer lying-down exercises.'

This early link with Miss Stansfeld and the P.T. College has been maintained and to this day students come with the latest ideas to pass on.

In any Senior school today, the timetable is a matter of long and complex organisation, since subjects are taught mainly by specialists. In the 1880s the class teacher was responsible for most subjects and for negotiating a timetable with the specialists, who could be very awkward.

Current affairs were not neglected; the death of Wilhelm I of Germany in 1888 demanded an essay. Without doubt, the Golden and Diamond Jubilees of Queen Victoria were celebrated, not least by an extra day's holiday.

The belief that education for girls must include certain socially desirable accomplishments is seen in the high degree of importance given to elocution, poetry speaking and singing. In the latter, the staff were expected to take part, especially in the entertainment of parents at the end of the Summer terms. The school academic year began in January, as the Cambridge Local Examinations were taken in the September term.

There were, as yet, no organised games, no school library and no free public library in the town. The girls walked or came by train from the surrounding villages. They wore buttoned boots and quite elaborate dresses, with pinafores and house slippers indoors. There was no uniform. They wrote with steel-nibbed pens, so easily crossed or broken, and a 'good hand' was very important to any girl hoping to go into business. Text books were to our minds dull and uninteresting. It was no wonder that girls thought up many naughty pranks, though discipline was strict. It was an age when parents and teachers expected to rule, and obedience was enforced by punishment.

To St. Paul's Square

The Summer term of 1892 saw the girls established in the old Grammar School buildings in St. Paul's Square. The handsome three-storeyed block topped by an elegant cupola surmounted by a cross, had been built originally for the Grammar School (Bedford School) and in the three months before the girls moved in, there had been a flurry of necessary alterations. Some of the Governors had objected to the Headmistress's room having to be reached through the gymnasium from the main building. Miss Porter replied to this criticism by remarking that the girls normally saw the Headmistress at break, not in lesson times, and that her room was accessible from the playground and gymnasium, where the girls played in wet weather. Moreover, such a position would enable the Headmistress to supervise divisions taken by student teachers and to check any idling in the dressing rooms, and to see how the student teachers did their work. An attempt to provide a dining room for the country girls failed at this early stage because the surveyor reported that the outbuilding suggested was not fit for the purpose.

Doubtless Miss Porter and her staff felt that they had a more independent existence now that they no longer shared buildings with the much more successful High School. They were pleased with the alterations made and looked forward to having the walls coloured with distemper during the Christmas holidays. There was no doubt that the new situation had much to commend it; a central position, readily accessible from both railway stations; a splendid view across the river and to St Paul's Church, and sufficient space for expansion.

That was the snag; after reaching a peak of 186 in May 1890, numbers were declining and were to continue to do so till Miss Porter retired. Partly this was caused by the existing scholarship systems, whereby girls already in the High School had a better chance of success than others. Miss Porter wrote that the questions in Botany (her especial grievance) and 'other subjects for the exam. are set by and marks awarded by the mistress who teaches the subject at the High School. If Botany is taken by an outsider no information is given as to the branch of it in which they would be examined.' If this seems a little defeatist, we must remember that Miss Porter had worked for ten years against a background of social and academic problems related to the subordinate view of the school commonly held. Finances were quite difficult; fees very low. England at the beginning of the 1890s was very strongly class conscious; Bedford, with its high proportion of military families seeking cheap schools for their sons, was deeply divided between the middle class incomers and the old established artisans. Local opinion was opposed to the idea of the Trust running two competing schools for girls, as they had come to do for boys.

The argument that the fees at B.G.M.S. were too high for the modest artisans whom it was designed to serve, is perhaps borne out by a glance at the occupations of parents of the girls entering in 1892–93. By no means all are recorded, but there are daughters of a fitter, butcher, travellers, timber merchants, dairyman, poultry farmer, tailor, grocers, photographer, baker, head gardener and builder, all of whom might be considered to be 'in trade', while on the other hand, there were children of a Colonel, a Mathematics master at B.M.S., farmers, an engineer and a Baptist minister, who were perhaps attracted by the fees being lower than at the High School, and who might consider themselves socially above the 'trading' classes. Fees of any kind were enough to close the doors to the vast majority of the poorer classes, especially at a time when legislation had made elementary education not only compulsory, but also free.

The first meeting of parents and scholars took place in the old Grammar School Hall on 15th July 1892, when Lady Isabella Whitbread presented the certificates. 'A well-arranged concert was given, opening with a pianoforte solo. . . . The second item, *The Rosy Morn* was contributed by singing classes I and II and was followed by a recitation of *The Loss of the Birkenhead* in which forms IIA and IIB distinguished themselves. . . . The principal item of the programme, so far as the pupils were concerned, was the cantata *Orpheus and Eurydice*, rendered in a praiseworthy manner. . . .'

The social afternoon continued with presentation of bouquets and compliments all round for the commodious school rooms which the girls had so prettily decorated with flowers. Five girls received their Cambridge Certificates, and the parents then dispersed to view the buildings and admire the Headmistress's watercolour sketches, and the pencil drawings of the pupils.

The same copy of the local paper which reported this meeting also records a little of the lives of some of Bedfordshire's less fortunate young people. Lucy White, a domestic servant, was accused by her employer, who farmed at Stagsden, of stealing 1s in money, a gold ring and other articles to the value of £2, and pleaded guilty. Her mother said it was her first situation and that the articles were laid out to tempt her. A lenient employer declined to press the case and Lucy was bound over for six months. Lucy was probably under 14 when this happened. How much happier the 146 girls at school, learning to sing or recite, and practising their cantata for the end of term parents' meeting.

Miss Porter continued to keep her record of new pupils and the class lists show the steady progress of girls up the school, but there are no more entries in her log book. At the end of 1892 each class list is annotated with the familiar formulae 'up', 'up conditionally' or 'no'; there are the usual number 'away for health' and one death recorded. The termly totals of girls in each form and in the school as a whole seemed to become more difficult to manage and Miss Porter's erasures increase in number. The V form remained small. Quite unusually, Miss Porter made notes in the register book for the Spring term 1894; Ethel Langley had whooping cough, Margaret Goodliff should have private lessons with Miss Turner; Lily Creeth would need help in French before September when she would go into IIIB; Clarice Lodge would be away all the term 'for health'. The numbers in the classes differed greatly; while Miss Brunton had 13 in Form I, young Miss Clara Porter, only one year out of Bedford Kindergarten Training College with a first class certificate, had 22 in IIB. IIA was larger with 28 girls and Miss Thomlinson. Miss Smith, now one of the old established teachers, had 32 girls in IIIB; IIIA was 24 in number, but the IV form only 12 and V, upper and lower, totalled 9 girls under the redoubtable Miss Crabtree. There were two student teachers who had some classes with the V form.

Miss Porter's retirement

On 9th March 1894, the Clerk to the Governors wrote his usual account of the quarterly meeting of the Governors of the Girls' Schools to Miss Porter. Paragraph 4 stated rather coldly 'that the resignation of the Headmistress of the Modern School be accepted and that the Chairman be asked to acknowledge the receipt of Miss Porter's letter and to make a suitable reply thereto'. All this between a note about the salary grant for the next year, and one about the proportion of fees to be paid in cases of absence through illness or exposure to infection. There is no comment in the log-book and no suggestion of a reason.

For 12 years Miss Porter had steered the school through its hazardous days; in two different buildings she had organised its classes, wrestled with problems of heating and decoration; she had set academic standards, kept down expenses, fought running battles over relationships with the High School, with the Governors and some of the town's worthies. At first, the ladies of her staff had a very restricted life, and she tried to help them by inviting them to a fortnightly Friday 'social' at which she read educational books to them while they crocheted. In the autumn she would tell them of her travels in Italy and Germany, and display the paintings she brought back with her. Of other entertainment, she and her staff found little until the Bedford Library offered a place to read, and, in the nineties, cycling made the younger teachers' lives much more joyful. There was, as yet, no school field, no theatre in the town and salaries were too low to permit jaunts to London.

Now in her late fifties, she retired from professional work but retained her interest in women's education. She became an Associate Member of the A.H.M., a privilege which seems to have been granted to few, as they were supposed to resign from the Association on retirement or resignation from work. In the early 1900s she wrote a letter to the *Daily Chronicle* in reply to an article which stated that the high school movement 'was hailed with joy in its beginning'. 'As one of the pioneers in the movement,' declared Miss Porter, 'I beg to differ . . . We had to strive for years against continual opposition . . . I have grounds for thinking that the work of the present Headmistresses is of a higher character than that of the former generation, for we, alas! did not enjoy the advantages which they have had in preparation for their work.'

She died very suddenly at Barnet on 9th February 1905, at the age of 69. Her obituary in the *Bedfordshire Times* notes her as the eldest daughter of Mr Joseph Long Porter and refers to the active part she played in 'social and other movements' while in Bedford, and the papers which she 'occasionally read before the local societies on subjects of interest to women'.

Of her character and personality we have little direct evidence. By the time she came to Bedford she had had more than twenty years' experience as a headmistress at six different schools; she was the first headmistress of at least four of these. In many ways she was a real pioneer, ready to meet the challenge of opposition and difficulties, with high ideals, hard-working and meticulous, though at times impatient with uninformed opposition. By the author of *The Forgotten Benson*, an unpublished biography of Ada McDowall, the first High School Headmistress, she is described as 'formidable, even forbidding, but also kind.'

The school owes much to Miss Porter; without her, it might well not have survived the opening years.

An Assured Position 1894–1914

Miss Dolby's appointment

When Miss Dolby replied to the advertisement of the position of Headmistress, sending in 30 printed copies of her testimonials, she had already been teaching for 10 years at Manchester High School, and was a qualified mathematician, having studied at Newnham College, Cambridge. She was among six ladies short-listed and called to attend the Quarterly Meeting of the Governors of the Girls' Schools in June 1894. She was appointed, and wrote out in the Minute Book her acceptance of the position, in the firm hand of the day. Edith Emily Dolby was 31, and she had found her life work. A staff photograph of 1897 shows her as a serious woman, dark haired, with regular features; her dress simple, a long light-coloured skirt and striped blouse, with leg o'mutton sleeves and tiny frill above a dark tie, a tight striped waist belt. Most of the staff wear variations on the same theme – the accepted fashion of the day for the teacher.

The Bedford to which she came was still a small town – some 51,000 inhabitants. It was already famous for its educational facilities and in addition to the Trust Schools, there were at least seven private schools for girls. The streets were quiet; only the carriers' carts and occasional carriage or bicycle disturbed the dust. The two railway stations offered easy access to London, the Midlands and East Anglia, and the town itself was pleasantly surrounded by farmlands and woods. St. Paul's Square could be described as a 'quiet spot' and the school enjoyed an enviable position in it. The playground ran down to the river, and was borrowed annually by the boys' schools for regatta parties. Across the river the rooks built in the elm trees near a timber yard.

In the wider world of politics, Mr Gladstone was, for the fourth time, Prime Minister and Irish Home Rule the issue of the day; the Russian Fleet sailed for the Far East, to be destroyed by the rising power of Japan; Africa was being divided up by the Western Colonial powers and Queen Victoria, the grandmother of most European monarchs, was moving steadily towards her Diamond Jubilee. The British Empire had reached its peak of power and self-confidence.

This had given an assurance to the boys' schools; they knew their purpose. They existed, like dozens of others in England, to produce the administrators and soldiers who would devote their lives at home and abroad to the development of this great Imperial heritage. The role of the girls' schools was less clear. In spite of Florence Nightingale and Elizabeth Garrett Anderson, there were few professions open to women, and the typewriter was only beginning to create the opportunities for 'office work' which ultimately transformed the prospects of many girls. In 1894, all too many were destined for a limited and limiting social round, and many parents still feared that too much education would reduce a girl's matrimonial chances. To be an 'old maid' was a truly terrible fate and to be avoided at all costs.

Her philosophy of education

Miss Dolby was convinced that education for girls should be aimed not at cramming, nor social accomplishments, but at fitting them for life in the present. 'We may think,' she said at her first end-of-year parents' meeting, 'with longing and regret of our grandmothers and great-grandmothers in their dainty flowered gowns and laces and ruffles, delicately strewing their household linen with lavender from the quaint old garden or occupied mysteriously in the still-room, and with these we associate ideas of a sweet graciousness and gentle charm and peace which we seem to miss in many of our girls today . . . we cannot turn back the closed page of history, even though a past age may seem to us more fascinating than our own; and to educate a girl on the lines which were found tolerably satisfactory even fifty years ago would most assuredly not be to prepare her for the inevitable battle before her. The great temptation is to regard education as synonymous with the acquisition of knowledge and skill in accomplishments. . . .' While writers deplored the illogicality of the female thought, most serious study was considered too heavy for girls. The growing number of subjects which could be taught made rigid selection necessary. 'Indeed', she continued, 'it is absolutely necessary to make a choice of subjects, and in making it, we must keep before us the end of true education – not so much to impart knowledge as to train all the faculties so that the pupil may be in the very best condition to acquire knowledge for itself. And lastly, I remind you all that any education worthy of the name must be the slow and laborious work of years; it is most truly a case of "precept upon precept, line upon line, here a little, there a little".' And she pleaded for girls to stay on at school till they were 17, so that they might benefit to the full from their schooldays.

There is in this a philosophy of education which we can uphold and develop today, and a lively personality which was to inspire the school from the moment of her coming.

New developments

Setting on one side Miss Porter's half abandoned logbook, Miss Dolby started a new book in a business-like manner with pages devoted to the number of pupils each term, and the names and salaries of staff. She maintained the existing silence as to Miss Porter's resignation and noted her own coming objectively. Then the changes began. 'Drill, Book-keeping, Euclid and Algebra and Botany', were at once made part of the usual curriculum. It is a mixed list but it reflects both a scientific and a practical approach and must have caused considerable perturbation among the staff, for we read 'Misses Brunton and Lister left at Christmas owing to changes made in work, also Miss Truchet. Miss Page from the Cambridge Training College came to take over Form I and to be in charge of Swedish Drill and Singing', while Miss Dolby herself took the V Form.

That first winter the elements seemed against the school. In the Autumn term the Ouse flooded the gymnasium and the passage to it, and though the school was only sent home for one half day, the gymnasium was out of action until the floor level was raised in the holidays and thereafter, to the disappointment of the young, the river was denied access to the building. After Christmas, there was a severe frost; all the water pipes froze and the river itself was frozen over for weeks, but school went on, while the playground was hacked up and the plumbers were kept busy.

A Hockey Club was founded and about 66 girls joined. The problem was acquiring a field, and for years different ones, most not very suitable, were hired. In the summer, a tennis court was marked out on the asphalt of the school playground. A subscription of 1s a term was taken and the girls made full use of this facility.

This increasing interest in physical education did not impede the drive towards achieving better academic standards. Form V took the College of Preceptors' Examination with good results. Two girls gained Northampton County Council Scholarships. Nearly one hundred took the Royal Drawing Society examinations and about seventy entered for the examinations of the 'Association for the Improvement of Plain Needlework', which involved making flannel petticoats, pillow cases and pinafores. Standards were high and in Grade III, in which only 9 out of 26 passed, Miss Dolby notes 'some mistakes were made as to the stitches required'. A more light hearted approach to the subject prevailed at the end of term when 'the girls were asked to dress dolls or do a piece of fancy work for competition in June; the work was excellent and I gave five prizes'. Perhaps the dolls were displayed, as well as the examined garments, when parents went over the school after the annual social afternoon.

Soon Miss Dolby had organised a boarding house at 46 Chaucer Road and opened a Sewing Meeting for Dr Barnardo's Homes on Saturday afternoons and a Dramatic Reading Society for Friday evenings. Holiday work seems to have taken the form of learning poems and reading, but interest in original work was stimulated by the production in manuscript of a first magazine, *The Eaglet*, in April 1896.

There were other excitements; Thursday half holidays for the virtuous who had not accumulated Conduct Marks or Returned Lessons; a picnic in the woods at Woburn Sands and at the end of term a visit to Cambridge for the V Form. One can picture the thrill of the train journey, the visits to colleges and libraries, lunch and tea at Miss Collier's invitation at Newnham and then the evening journey back to Bedford. In the autumn a Dancing class was inaugurated and a Cookery class at the School of Cookery limited to 10 pupils, at a fee of 2s 6d ($12\frac{1}{2}$p) for 6 lessons. The Autumn term 1896 ended with a grand concert at the Town Hall, at which the Mayor (Mr G. Wells) and the Duchess of Bedford spoke of the progress made since Miss Dolby's arrival and the certificates were distributed. The accounts for this event survive in Miss Dolby's hand.

Expenses for Concert

	£	s.	d.
For Town Hall (one rehearsal)	2	10	0
Tea from Normans for 20	1	0	0
Man at Town Hall		6	0
Flowers and part bouquet		4	0
Piano		10	6
Maids		2	0
Smith for carpet, moving furniture, etc.		15	0
	5	7	6

It seems that this must have exceeded the amount allowed for it is followed by the note, '£1 2s 6d paid by E.E.D.' For the occasion programmes were printed by Timaeus of Bedford and the event was reported not only in the *Bedford Standard* and the *Daily News* but also in the *Buckingham Standard*, the latter on 26th December. The *Bedford Standard* was issued on Christmas Day! That very fact may seem amazing to us; the length of the proceedings would also shock us; six songs, three recitations, three orchestral pieces, a German playlet, a French dialogue, ten tableaux of nursery rhymes, two scenes from stories and a carol. No wonder there was hearty applause at the end. And fortunately, school broke up the next day, meeting specially on a Saturday to do so.

The turn of the century

1897 saw the Diamond Jubilee of Queen Victoria; a whole day's holiday on 22nd June gave girls and staff an opportunity to join in local celebrations, but national thanksgiving was to be short-lived, and the death of Mr Gladstone in 1898 was deeply felt. St. Paul's bell tolled his long years, slowly, while the girls in the North Block found it hard to concentrate as they realised that great changes must soon come about. Soon the Boer War began to darken the horizon, and anxieties about fathers posted to South Africa clouded happy days. Children came from South Africa, two whose parents had been through the siege of Mafeking. The school, like the nation, swung to violent rejoicing when that town was relieved and the Union Jack flags were proudly marked in on the big map in the gymnasium. The war was far away, and, apart from personal tragedies, had little effect on everyday life, but in January 1901 the whole country was shocked by the news of the Queen's death. A late arrival at the Staff Meeting had seen the placard announcing it, and next day the papers relayed the request for general mourning. Mistresses with free periods slipped out to the drapers and milliners for black hats, gloves, crêpe veils; most at that time would have a black skirt or dress, for the wearing of black for the deaths of even distant relations was socially imperative. Miss Buckley, who had recently joined the staff, remembered that one agitated fellow teacher wore her hard black sailor hat with the price ticket dangling from it. The newspapers vied with each other in the width of their black borders; all private notepaper was edged in black and the Harpur Trust used black edged-paper for its clerk's usual communications with Miss Dolby. Never again was a nation so to externalise its grief. Eighteen months later the school broke up early to celebrate the end of the Boer War.

These years, from Diamond Jubilee to the coming of peace again, marked a real watershed; it is seldom that the 'turn of the century' is historically significant, but a new spirit seemed to be in the air as the motor car took to the roads, and Edward VII revived a forgotten version of kingship.

For the Girls' Modern School, too, it was a good time. Numbers were climbing steadily; more girls stayed on into the V form; more girls successfully took the Oxford Senior examinations and were placed in Class 1. It became possible to award an annual scholarship to cover the last three years' fees, and one can trace the winners going on to obtain their Senior Local Certificates.

Joan Langley, who won the scholarship in 1897, commended by the examiner for work that 'showed great merit, intelligence and accuracy, especially in Arithmetic, Euclid and French', obtained a Division 1 pass in the Junior Oxford examination in the following year and passed the Senior Oxford in 1900, winning in the same year a two year scholarship to the High School.

Five members of staff came in these years, who, between them, gave 164 years of service, and with Miss Dolby and Miss Smith they formed a stable nucleus for the school. The first to come was Miss Gillions, who had entered the school as a pupil, in 1883. Her reminiscences, set down in the Jubilee magazine, and her collection of O.G.A. leaflets and newspaper cuttings show what a lively and loyal person she was. She had enjoyed Scripture and Elocution lessons with Miss Porter, and had been inspired by the History and Literature classes taken by Miss Crabtree. Leaving school in December 1891, after taking her Cambridge Local Examination, she had immediately gone to France as Governess-companion for two happy years. Invited by an aunt to spend six months in Dresden, she applied herself to the study of German, painting, singing, music and embroidery. She went on to teach in Germany, and after five years abroad wrote to Miss Dolby, who, at that point, needed a mistress to take French and German. So came one of the most loved of all the B.G.M.S. staff.

The next to arrive was Miss Buckley, who succeeded Miss Crabtree as V form mistress, and specialised in History and Literature. She was to identify herself deeply with the school and particularly with the development of dramatic work and music. When ill health forced her to retire in 1928, the Old Girls of 30 years could scarcely imagine the school without her.

Then came Miss Coltman, Miss Hensman and, in 1901, Miss Crump. Miss Hensman was appointed to teach Science in 1900, Miss Coltman came in mid-term to take III Upper, whose former teacher left to be married, and Miss Crump took over Form I in the Spring term, after training for Kindergarten work at Cheltenham. With them, and much their senior, was Miss Smith, whose 40 years of service is almost unequalled, and who was the great link with the very beginning of the school.

During these years there was constant growth; new forms

Miss M. E. Porter,
First Headmistress 1882–94.

Miss E. E. Dolby, 1894–1926.

Miss B. A. Tonkin, 1926–46.

Miss I. L. Forster, 1946–55.

The Headmistress and Staff in 1897, *see page 26.*

A class of 1900, II Lower, *see page 38.*

A class of 1903, see page 37.

The Headmistress and Staff in 1914, see page 38.

A view of the St.Paul's Square building.

The Gymnasium.

The Science Room.

A Cookery class, see page 66.

The houses in Cardington Road.

The great flood of 1947.

The Abbey, Cardington Road.

A procession entering St. Paul's for service, 1952.

were started; orchestra practice was held under Miss Buckley's baton; Miss Dolby gave parties for the school, recalled years afterwards with nostalgic delight. The custom of performing French and German playlets at the Certificate Distribution continued; tennis tournaments were held. The perennial problem of cold classrooms was dealt with in 1899 by having a 'Hot Water Apparatus' fixed in six classrooms and corridors. The link with Dr Barnardo's was maintained and parcels of garments made in the holidays were sent. In that year the Governors found it necessary to remind the Headmistresses of the two girls' schools that 'an escort satisfactory to the Headmistress shall be provided for the boarders on their way to and from school, at the place of worship attended by them, during their hours of exercise and at such time other than the school hours when they are not in the Boarding House' and to remind Headmistresses that the Harpur Trust Schools are undenominational. As a copy of this resolution was to be sent to the Bedford Free Church council, we may imagine that they had made some protest – or had the girls been a little too high-spirited? Perhaps they made up for it later by contributing to the Children's Penny Fund for homes for soldiers and sailors.

Miss Dolby was encouraged by the annual congratulation of the Governors on the examination successes and general efficiency of the school. She continued her efforts to keep abreast of new developments. An optional shorthand class was introduced, and apparatus, including ropes, provided for the gym. Additional help in Science was given when Miss Shore came over from Cambridge once a fortnight to give practical instruction.

From 1902 to 1914, the last years of the old order, the England of rigid class distinction, of 'Upstairs, Downstairs', of Imperial glory, passed all too quickly. They were patterned by the heralds of a new way of life and thought; the growth of the Independent Labour Party, the changing role and increased power of the Trade Unions, the growing violence of the campaign for Women's Suffrage. (For many years a Suffragette banner hung over the balcony in The Dame Alice School Hall.) Other changes came; the first Old Age Pensions ('the Lloyd George', as many grateful recipients called their 5s (25p) a week), the development of County Secondary Schools and responsibility of County Councils for education, a growing awareness of social needs, and the dawning of realisation that poverty is not, of itself, a crime. In the wider world, vast patterns of alliances were being formed by statesmen whose avowed purpose was peace, but whose methods would ultimately engulf the world in war. A few realised the increasing tensions as crisis followed crisis, but for the majority, danger was far away. Bank Holidays were a novel excitement, and the horizon was limited to their own town and their own class.

Formation of VI form

The school had at this time entered on a period of success and prosperity. Numbers increased to a peak of 312 in January 1908; it became possible for girls to stay on over the age of 17 years and in 1910 Miss Dolby, for the first time, notes the formation of a VI form. This late development of the academic senior work which had for so long left the school without a clear cut aim, produced a great increase in confidence from this time onwards. It was this which made such a difference in the history of the two girls' schools, since the High School, from its inception, was able to establish an academic reputation which rapidly became nationwide.

Many improvements were undertaken, from the acquisition of a permanent school field in Chaucer Road, where a pavilion was erected, to the introduction of a wider variety of activities; cricket and rounders vied with the established tennis and hockey, and swimming led to the annual races and competitions, both for individuals and forms. Hockey and tennis matches were played against Bedford Ladies, the P.T. College, teams at Wellingborough, St. Ives, Hitchin and Higham Ferrers. The school owed a great deal to its connection with the Physical Training College, and Miss Stansfeld and her staff helped in innumerable ways, so that the most up-to-date ideas and developments were quickly passed on.

A strong movement towards the improvement of science teaching in girls' schools developed during these years, and in 1904 the Science and Art rooms were fitted up. The provision of proper benches, sinks, the familiar Bunsen burners and glass apparatus made possible the first experimental work and this was followed in 1914 by the building and equipping of the Botany Laboratory.

Expansion – the new buildings

The growth in numbers led to a series of temporary measures; a room was hired in the Y.M.C.A. building at a cost of £20 p.a. for rent, coal, gas and cleaning, and Form II Middle were installed there. As Miss Gillions remembered at the Jubilee – 'The traffic was not so dangerous as it is now (1932) but getting a large class of lively infants safely backwards and forwards after prayers and at break was an anxious task. It is breathless work to reach the top of the building here, after the many stairs, but you can imagine what one felt like on arriving at Room No. 19 which was a flight higher still! Underneath then, as now, was a pork butcher's shop and once a week my French lesson was given to the accompaniment of piercing shrieks from unfortunate pigs somewhere down below, which was not exactly helpful.' Then came the new building. In 1909 a second floor was added to the old South Block and the archway and new classrooms beyond were built. Now the school had a beautiful and purpose-built riverside block, and generations of Bedford Girls were to look back with fondness on happy days spent there. The building was designed by Mr Young and built by Fosters who had erected the first girls' school in Bromham Road.

Miss Buckley remembered, long afterwards, the difficulties of the building period, when the staff were without a Common Room and put their outdoor garments and corrected books in the passage by the old Art Room, keeping warm by the stove which always smelt of Brunswick Black. There was one period when 150 girls had to use half of one of the large classrooms as a dressing room, and pegs and boot holes lined all the corridors. Even the gymnasium was pressed into service as a classroom, and some forms had to manage to concentrate while two lessons went on in one room. As the rooms became available they were put into immediate use, so no formal opening ceremony took place, but the concert and presentation of certificates, postponed from the previous December, gave, on a cold June day, an opportunity for parents and friends to view the new buildings.

The *Bedfordshire Times and Independent* of 11th June 1909, devoted $2\frac{1}{2}$ columns to the new building and gives us a detailed description of the work which was displayed to the parents. It is worthy of quotation. 'All the classrooms were bright and gay with flowers in the windows, groups of flowers in the fireplaces . . . with here and there little collections of natural history specimens, materials for object lessons and examples of artistic work, whether of the brush, the needle or the rolling pin . . . In the Science Room, benches were fitted up for experimental work in Chemistry and Physics . . . on one bench were shown floral diagrams drawn or built up of the actual parts of the flowers by the younger students . . . There were exquisite botanical studies of such subjects as the barley grass, with its spikelet and awns exactly delineated on a magnified scale . . . Teaching specimens of fruits and seeds, illustrating methods of dispersal and other points are preserved in little boxes or in bottles of spirit . . .

'A number of maps, very neatly drawn and tinted, being the ordinary classwork were also shown. One admirable piece of work is Muriel Crummie's History Chart embellished with charming little pen and ink sketches . . .

In other classrooms "our expert" was enabled to study the needlework in its varied branches and admire the drawn-thread table cover made by J. Wallace and the Hardanger work of E. Baxter, both these experts having attained the mature age of 12, also the ribbon work on muslin by E. Staniford aged 13 . . .

'The art of cookery was exemplified by a most enticing array of orange cakes, sausage rolls, fillets of plaice, Swiss rolls, milk loaf, meat pie, chocolate mould and other confections, not forgetting the loaf of household bread made by Ruth Collier and one of wholemeal bread by Irene Underhill. These loaves had a most excellent appearance. The housewife who can make bread at home will be an acquisition in the times of dear bread which are said to be looming ahead . . .

'In the Art room the exhibition was of the most interesting nature, particularly as regards the original designs for decoration of dessert plates, table centres, candle shades, d'oyleys and menu cards . . .

'The school hall which is also used for physical education was on this occasion the tea room where the guests were entertained at numerous little tables amid most cheerful surroundings. Groups of plants, bright nosegays and a copious display of the national flag on the walls presented a scene which was all the more stimulating by reason of the music of the band from the terrace without, where the parapet was draped in crimson festooned over in white fabrics fastened with deep blue rosettes.'

'Hence – 'tis but a step to the new buildings . . . suffice now to say that the rooms are unusually lofty, well lighted, carefully ventilated and comfortably warmed in winter. The room for the I Form was showing the paper folding, pretty little clay figures and other kindergarten work of the little girls.'

We can almost hear the proud Mamas as they move so elegantly from room to room, aware of their fashionable dresses and elaborate hats, wishing perhaps that the weather had been kinder, for the temperature would not have been discreditable to the month of February.

So the school reached its definitive architectural form on this site, and its new classrooms with their sunny views across the river and the gracious bay windows of the Head's and Staff's rooms became a part of the river frontage of Bedford. The cost of the new building had been shared by the Harpur Trust and the County Council who appreciated the work being done for both Borough and County. At this time nearly one-third of the girls came from outside the borough, and the school, with its strong emphasis on domestic economy, was providing for many needs. At this time, Mr Howard, Chairman of the Governors, announced that £50 was to be voted for leaving exhibitions and that in subsequent years the sum would be £100, to provide two exhibitions to be held at colleges or universities.

Personalia – in word and picture

These pre-war years saw a great interest in photography and several sets of form photographs survive from them. In 1903 a handsome embossed album was used to hold a series of form photographs. The twelve little girls in Form I sit and stand around the young and attractive Miss Crump. Her dress is heavily braided and she wears the fashionable high lace vest at the throat. Her pupils are in frocks gathered into high yokes, frilled and lacy, or more primly attired in dark skirts, just below the knee and wide-collared blouses; all have long sleeves; all wear black woollen stockings and black shoes. Two of these eight-year-olds are in mourning and wear black armbands. The children's hair is long and flows from a variety of bows worn at the back or top of the head. Eyes screwed up against the sun, and frozen into immobility for and by the camera, they nevertheless seem as though in a moment the silence will be broken and a high spirited little group will clatter back to lessons. At the top of the school, Form V poses with Miss Buckley. Pince-nez in place, high necked light blouse, her dark hair swept back, controlled and unsmiling, she is surrounded by a dozen pupils, three of whom were pupil teachers. All wear full-length skirts, some tucked or flounced or braided. Their blouses vary from the severe to the frilly, but all are long sleeved and high collared. Only their hands and faces emerge from the all enveloping clothing. Hair shows as many styles as girls. All of it is long, ranging from the frankly loose and bouffant to the severely smooth and neatly tied back. They look so earnest, yet there is a watchful twinkle in the eyes, and surely the elaborate pendant and fob watch suggest that 'best' clothes were the order of the day for the photographer.

In between are larger classes, some a bit fuzzy where a fidgety miss could not keep still for the camera. All look to our eyes wildly overdressed, and among the sailor collars and lace yokes, the first gym dresses appear, pleated on to stitched yokes and worn with lighter blouses. How hot these high necked blouses must have been, many of them buttoned right up to the chin; how neat the belted waistlines.

A few years later the staff make their bow, posed against the ivied wall, seated on some of the newly acquired garden seats. The style is more severe; many of the blouses have stiffened collars and short ties, the skirts, varying in fabric and colour, are floor length and the hemlines are stiffened and probably brush braided. There is nothing frivolous about them, but there is a sense of purpose and of standard. Another photograph taken indoors in the art room presents a more severe version, but delights with the background of mounted drawings and quite extraordinary plaster casts that deck the walls. The exposure must have been longer, and the faces are more set with the effort of keeping so still, but they are undeterred by difficulties.

Gradually the more flamboyant dress disappears for the girls and the gym tunic takes over. Even this did not mean uniform, for everyone was different, one even boasting cape sleeves to the tunic. Probably this was the result of the emphasis on physical activities and the influence of Miss Stansfeld.

Determination and ability led to the first major academic successes. Winifred Collier, having successfully taken the Oxford Senior Local Examination in July 1903, and the Cambridge Higher Local in 1904, went up to Newnham in the following year and completed her Mathematics Tripos. In 1906 Kathleen Plumbridge gained the Silver Medal for Geography in the Oxford Senior Local Examination and in 1907, two girls, Violet Driver and Margery Stansfield, went up to Royal Holloway College, Margery with a College Bursary. Both girls had gained 1st Class Honours Certificates in Oxford Senior Locals in 1906, with distinctions, Violet in Religious Knowledge and Margery in German. Margery gained B.A. German Hons. Annie Maden, who passed her Senior Local Examination in 1909 and 1910 and then held a Northants. Scholarship, gained exemption from Matriculation, and was awarded one of the first leaving exhibitions and a County Scholarship of £20. She entered Edinburgh Medical School in 1910 where she had a most successful career, winning prizes and medals and obtaining the M.B. and Ch.B. She held the post of Senior Demonstrator of Anatomy in the Women's Medical School and during the Great War 1914–18 she was R.M.O. at the Royal Hampshire Hospital in Winchester.

From 1910 success increased. In that year, 27 candidates entered and all passed in the Senior Oxford Examinations; in 1912 13 gained 11 distinctions and 10 Honours Certificates. The school no longer entered girls for the Junior Examination, having gained confidence in its own tests, no longer needing to reassure parents by external junior papers. Distinctions were gained in Botany, Geography, Religious Knowledge and Literature; each year many gained exemption from Matriculation. Art was a strong subject too; Kathleen Easmon gained an exhibition of £20 and free tuition at South Kensington School of Art awarded by the L.C.C. and in the next year M. Sedgwick gained a scholarship of £50 for 2 years awarded by Leicester School of

Art. Maud Sargent gained the South Kensington Art Class Teachers' Certificate, and was highly commended by the R.D.S. for her watercolours; she already held a full certificate with Honours in all 6 divisions and had had many drawings exhibited by the R.D.S.

Hilda Johnston, who gained a 1st class in Oxford Senior Locals went on to London University. E. Jeffrey won a Gillott Scholarship at Whitelands. P. Horton gained her B.A. at Manchester in 1913. Edith Creamer gained 1st Classes in Botany, Zoology and Physics in her Liverpool University Intermediate exams.

In 1914, the third O.G.A. leaflet tells of Old Girls' successes. Violet Driver was by then teaching in Exeter. Gertrude Boyd was Secretary to the Master of Rotunda Hospital, Dublin; L. Gilham was teaching near Cardiff, Agnes Lack at the Royal School for the Deaf and Dumb in Margate, Kathleen Ponting, Gladys Brickdale, Alice Dawes, Edith Brookbank and Gertrude Davey were nursing or training for it. Lily Howard was teaching in a mission school in Kobe, Japan. Others teaching were Margery Stansfield and Lizzie Ivens but Ruth Hendry had taken up dairy work and gone to Ireland.

The formation of the Old Girls' Association in 1911 marked another step in the corporate consciousness of the school. Miss Dolby had been opposed to the formation of such a society until she was convinced by the enthusiasm and efficiency of Marjorie Howard that there was sufficient support. Marjorie had passed her Senior Oxford in 1904 and was living in the High Street, Bedford, still at that time a residential area. The preliminary meeting was held in the gymnasium on 30th June 1911; Miss Dolby was chosen as President, Marjorie Howard was Secretary and Miss Gillions became Vice-President and Treasurer; a Committee of 12 was elected to assist them. The subscription was fixed at 2s (10p) p.a. (1s for overseas members) and by 1916 a life subscription was organised. One general meeting a year and a summer reunion, if possible, were to be held. The first two were held in the B.M.S. hall and the third at school. All had serious lectures to start with – a talk by the Assistant Secretary of the Central Bureau for the Employment of Educated Girls, and another on 'Openings for Educated Women in the Colonies'. The Association has continued ever since and its leaflets present an unbroken record of the doings of Old Girls from 1911 to the present day. It has been served by a series of loyal and gracious officers and has provided a link between the generations of school leavers and happy reunions for many lively 'Old Girls'.

Let Kathleen Ashwell (*née* Custance) conclude this pre-war period for us. 'Recalling memories,' she writes, 'I came to school either in 1910 or 1911 and was put into II Lower at half term, Miss Jones being Form Mistress. They were halfway through a long poem about the battle of Naseby and at top of the page were the words, "Stout Skippon hath a wound, the centre hath given ground" – I forget the rest!

'Of course I remember school concerts; how well I remember the first time getting on to the stage and seeing the curtains drawn and Miss Buckley coming on and giving us all a beaming smile; she had always looked so stern when I saw her at school.' Separated by two world wars, and all the multitudinous changes of the period since, the message rings clear. 'It was a happy school; individuals counted (dear Miss Gillions took our German class and she was kind enough to lend me her music copy of *The Erl King*), and the work done has been a treasury of the mind ever since.'

The First World War and After

The First World War

For the Girls' Modern School as for most of Britain, 1914 came with nothing to show its epoch-making nature. In the Christmas holidays electric light had been installed in almost all the rooms, a great improvement on the hissing gas lamps of the past. The Spring term passed uneventfully; the Old Girls' meeting was held in January, with music and dancing for about 100 members, a lecture on Dr Barnardo's Homes, with lantern slides, took place in February; the hockey teams had a successful season. The Summer term passed in the usual welter of examinations and competitions. The log-book would suggest that there was equal enthusiasm and determination for both.

While the last tidying up of the Summer term progressed, the lamps were going out over Europe, into a darkness which no one at the time could even imagine. The term ended on 25th July. It was the day on which Serbia replied to the Austrian ultimatum after the murder of Archduke Franz Ferdinand. Three days later Austria declared war, and those alliances made years before took effect, to plunge all Europe into war, like climbers roped together on some crumbling cliff dragging each other to destruction.

One girl who was at school throughout the war was Muriel Thompson (*née* Back). She writes of the excitements of life in the I Form, 'we could hardly wait to reach the Upper Third when we should be able to weigh morsels on the delicate scales ranged round the science room in glass cases. We were all looking forward to studying German, but that subject was discontinued as it was considered to be unpatriotic when we were at war with Germany, but we young things were imagining that we might be useful in catching a German spy if we had some knowledge of the language.

'Instead we could choose between furthering our study of Latin or taking a course in Commercial subjects, namely Shorthand and Book-keeping.

'No school dinners were provided but at morning break milk was available at 1d a glass, also a Swiss bun or a doughnut. These were served by Gilbert, the caretaker, who used to carry large scuttles of coal for the huge fires in the classrooms. (This must have been very tiring work, carried out uncomplainingly – in fact, I never remember hearing him speak.)

'The classrooms also each had one radiator at the back and the windows were always open, so we were very cold in winter and most people wore woollen mittens and, of course, long black cashmere stockings. Almost everyone suffered from chilblains on hands and feet, but these were accepted as inevitable.'

The school was lucky in that the work to build and fit up the Botany laboratory, popularly called the Greenhouse, was already in hand, and that the new desks had been ordered for the Geography room. Games sessions, however, suffered because the field could only be used when it was not required for military purposes.

As the news from the war became more frightening, with the German sweep through Belgium and towards Paris, the school began its voluntary service. 'Girls occupied in knitting belts, making extra Guild garments', notes Miss Dolby, 'Collection from 26th October on Mondays for Belgian Refugees' Fund'. It was no time for jollification or self-congratulation, and no school concert was held. Those extra Guild garments helped to fill the parcels which were sent for Christmas to Barnardo's Homes, St. Audrey's Homes, the Belgian Children's Treat and the families in need in Bedford. 240 toys and 282 garments, nearly all warm, had been collected. It was in line with the generosity which marked the school's Christmas giving throughout its first century.

It was 'business as usual' for staff and girls as the Western Front reeled under the hammer blows of the German advance, and every effort was made to keep a normal curriculum going. The examinations, the hockey matches and swimming races all took place as usual. The Charity collections tell poignantly of the direction to which all hearts turned. 'Weekly collection for 8 weeks sent to Beds. Regiment Prisoners of War Help Fund, £14 17s 0d. To Lady Hamilton for soldiers in Dardanelles, £1 2s 6d. Collection for "Our Day" Red Cross and St. John's Ambulance £10 11s 0d. Collection for wool for mufflers and mittens for War Office, men at front £14 15s 3d' – 61 mufflers and 60 pairs of mittens were knitted that summer term, ready for the winter.

School life in wartime

We have from Mrs Eva Cox (*née* Dickens) a vivid picture of a schoolgirl's life in the war days. She writes, 'When I entered Bedford Girls' Modern School in 1915 as a Harpur Trust scholar I stepped into a new world. I find it quite impossible to put into words what it meant to me to have my own books and writing materials in my own desk – timetables pinned on to the inside of the lid, song case, atlas and sermon paper in their outside compartment. And to begin a whole range of exciting new subjects! We bought our own books in those days, and scholarship girls received a grant for that purpose.

'Our school beside the river, next to the Shire Hall in St. Paul's Square had been the home of Bedford Grammar School which, just about then, became known as Bedford School. The stone stairs were much hollowed out by generations of feet rushing up and down them . . . an archway between the old and new buildings led to a gravelled path beside the river but this was out of bounds to all except the VI form.

'At first we wore straw boaters summer and winter, with a hat band in blue and light blue in a zig-zag design, but that was soon changed to a panama type hat with a band with horizontal stripes, and in winter to a felt hat. Later still, maybe because of wartime and post-war shortages, a rather unbecoming serge cap was introduced; fortunately VI form girls were excused from wearing these . . .

'Morning school ended at 12.50 and we all went home to dinner, returning at 2.30 and staying until 4.30. The boarders of course walked in crocodile and the train girls went to a somewhat frugal wartime meal at the Victory tea rooms over Braggins' shop. The only subjects taught in the afternoon were Singing, Drawing, Needlework, Science and Games. This latter took the whole afternoon as the school field was in Chaucer Road. Half of the other afternoons was spent doing 'prep' under supervision . . .

'The First World War coloured most of my schooldays. I remember so well the sound of the military bands passing over the Town Bridge on their way from the Barracks to the Cemetery. Many soldiers were under canvas at Howbury Hall near Goldington early in 1916 and there was an epidemic of measles leading to pneumonia and a number of deaths. I never hear Chopin's *Funeral March* without being transported in imagination to that prep. room. Another tune that takes me back to school is Elgar's *Pomp and Circumstance* March – the one to which *Land of Hope and Glory* is sung. At intervals throughout the war and of course at the Armistice, we assembled in the Hall to be told the news and to sing both that and Kipling's *Recessional* and, I feel sure, the National Anthem.'

The end of the Autumn term 1915 saw the annual concert revived with an ambitious programme of songs, piano solos, dances, and a dramatised French recitation. The certificates were distributed by Mrs Rowland Prothero. Fifteen candidates had entered and all passed their Oxford Senior Local Examinations; nine gained first class honours. Two girls, Ada Wesley and Ivy Hendry, had taken the London Matriculation Examination, and both were placed in division 1. It is clear that work of outstanding quality was being done both academically and artistically, as Silver and Bronze Stars were awarded for drawings exhibited by the R.D.S. Mrs Prothero's address to the girls was on the theme of the call to serve their country posed by the war. The call was being met. The painstaking sewing and knitting continued; collections were made for War Charities; the boarders gave a successful performance of the *Pirate of Ranora*, which helped to swell the sum raised to £50. A War Savings Association was begun, affiliated to the National War Savings Committee and various inducements were offered to encourage saving. 'Girls to have 3d when 5s saved', notes Miss Dolby. Old Girls were nursing in France, as well as in many English hospitals, others were working in munitions. (Ethel Davey, afterward Matron at St. Pancras Hospital, was one of the first twenty nurses who volunteered for the front.)

During the war years, the numbers in the school began to rise steadily, reaching 426 in September 1918 when 9 free places were offered to girls who had done well in the County Scholarship Examination, a new departure for the Trust. This gradual expansion resulted in the Headmistress's room being turned into a Sixth form room in 1916, while the Headmistress took over the office, a small room upstairs being used for the office. It was typical of the new attitudes forced upon people by the war, that when Miss Fish, who taught science, married, she remained on the staff as Mrs Dale. Numbers made it necessary to have a more formal office organisation, and in 1917 Miss Knight came as secretary and teacher of commercial subjects. She was to stay until April 1953, 36 years of devoted service. She soon became greatly beloved and deeply respected, an institution within the school, setting a standard of efficiency and courtesy which was remembered by all who came in contact with her. New classes were formed and temporary staff appointed, but the overcrowding was not really reduced until East Lodge was opened in September 1918 and the I and II forms were moved there, with adjusted hours, 9.15–12.45, 2.45–4.15, to allow for the extra distance out of town. East Lodge, now Dame Alice House, offered not only a number of new classrooms, but also a delightful garden with many mature beech and chestnut trees, lawns and shrubbery borders.

The First Royal Visit

While the work of preparing East Lodge was in progress, a royal visit, the most important social event of the school's history to date took place. It was planned at a time when the fortunes of war seemed at their blackest. The great German offensive of March 1918 had driven the Allies back to within 40 miles of Paris. Though preparations for a major counter-attack were in progress, in the nature of things this could not be public knowledge and, all that the people of Bedford knew, like the rest of England, was the constant demand for men to fill the trenches, and the pathetic streams of blue-clad wounded who returned from the front. Discharged ex-servicemen were employed in factories, such as Allens, alongside the hundreds of women whose labour was essential to the war effort. The royal visit was in the nature of a boost to production and morale as well as an acknowledgement of the educational work of the Harpur Trust. At Bedford School especially the emphasis would be on the O.T.C., and lorry loads of wounded men came to see their King. For the girls' schools, the occasion was educational in nature, though the Old Girls serving as V.A.D.s pointed a lesson for all. The whole town was involved, from the gaily decorated railway station to the Town Hall, via de Parys Avenue, 'the Champs Elysées of Bedford' as the *Bedfordshire Times* put it. Every church flew the Union Jack, hundreds of flags streamed out in the wind on that bright 27th June. The day was to be remembered by everyone present, both girls and staff, as the highlight of their experience. In an age before radio or television the King and Queen were unknown figures of distant mystique to most of their subjects, and few would ever have caught a glimpse of them before the great day.

In order to simplify matters for their Majesties, the High School building once more accommodated the two schools; the Modern School Girls in their prettiest summer frocks arrived and were deployed in a block of rooms which opened into each other, while Geography and Needlework lessons were demonstrated in adjoining classrooms. The long waiting time was relieved of tedium by singing, and practising the art of curtseying, and when at last the time came, the school launched into *Land of our Birth* with such rapt attention from the juniors in the front row that the King broke into laughter. He made a short speech and asked for a week's extra holiday before they moved on to see the Geography and Handwork. Such close contact with royalty was most exciting for the girls as the King and Queen moved between the rows of desks to examine the work displayed. Miss Dolby was, of course, presented and a photograph shows her with Miss Collie of the High School against a parade of V.A.D. nurses (Old Girls of the School) at the door of the High School.

Such gracious moments, scented with the fragrance of the shower bouquet of sweet peas matched in colour to the Queen's toque, remain vivid in memory.

The day to day work continued; the external examinations, examinations for the school Bursaries (won that summer by

Barbara Elvin and Joyce Jeremy). The new Cambridge Higher School Certificate, for girls who had already passed the Senior Local Examinations and were preparing for university, was passed by the Head Girl, Hilda Howe, who gained a distinction in French, and by Nellie Common, Annie Fitch and Mary Markham.

A Staff Pension Scheme

A major new departure was the institution of a pension scheme for mistresses; salaries of staff ranged at this time from £130–£200 p.a. and included a wartime bonus, introduced to help with rising prices. The war, in September obviously drawing to a close, had left a generation of women who would never have the opportunity of marriage, and who must provide for their own old age. It had been the custom of the Trust in centuries past to grant discretionary pensions to those who had grown old in its service, but this was no longer sufficient, and proper arrangements now had to be made. The matter had been under consideration for years. In 1910 the Governors had set up a committee to investigate the financial affairs of the two Girls' Schools with a view to the formation of a Pension Fund for the Assistant Mistresses, but at that time the necessary money was not available. Six years later a Committee was again set up, consisting of Mr Geoffrey Howard and Mr G. C. Walker, this time to formulate a Pension Scheme for Assistant Mistresses in the Modern School.

The Scheme set out the following points:

1 The pension shall be provided by such contributions from the Governors not exceeding in each case £20 p.a. as shall be necessary to provide a pension of £50 a year at the age of 55 or an equivalent endowment. If the annual premiums exceed £20 the additional amount shall be paid by the Mistress herself.

2 The pensions shall be provided by an insurance with the Scottish Provident Society for an Annuity of £50, the first half-yearly instalment to be payable on attainment of age 55 or an alternative cash payment of £730 at age 55.
The Annuity to be payable for five years certain with continuance thereafter during life.

The premiums paid to be returned with 3% compound interest in the event of death or surrender before age 55.

3 Retirement for those under the Scheme shall be compulsory at the end of the term in which the age of 55 is attained, but a Mistress may be continued in her appointment on the recommendation of the Head Mistress approved by the Governors for one year, and such recommendations may be repeated year by year until the end of the term in which the age of 60 is attained.

4 In the event of a Mistress leaving the School, the policy shall become her property, subject to such safeguards as may be hereinafter determined.

5 This scheme shall be compulsory on future appointments, but in the case of Mistresses already on the staff it shall be optional.

This scheme was to come into operation as soon as the Modern School was recognised by the Board of Education as eligible for Grant.

This question of a Board of Education grant also had a fairly long history. In 1912 arrangements were being made for a General Inspection of the school which was scheduled for May 1913 and the usual external examinations and inspections by the Oxford Delegacy were in that year confined to the highest form for award of the leaving Bursaries. On the strength of the Report the Governors decided to apply for the grant and to offer 25 per cent free places in order to comply with the Regulations. Before this could be implemented, the war had started and such a major decision was postponed for some two years, and then formal negotiations were started in January 1917, and by May 1918 the only question left was the date from which the Government Grant would be estimated. So the school attained the status of 'Direct Grant Grammar School' and the doors were opened to many girls who could not have afforded even the meagre fees of those days.

With the achievement of this change, the staff pension scheme was implemented; nine of the staff were insured at an annual cost of £171 10s 10d; Miss Buckley, Miss MacFarland and Miss Hensman increased their existing insurance policies by the £20 each paid by the Governors and the five not insured and unable to fulfil the conditions of the scheme (Miss A. M. Smith (aged 54), Miss C. Porter (aged 52), Mrs Dale (leaving), Miss A. Jones (aged 43) and Miss Gillions (aged 45)), were to have £20 p.a. invested in Consols for them. All new staff would have to join the scheme.

Almost immediately after this the mistresses 'on the permanent staff' held a meeting to elect a representative (lady) Governor. Miss Jex-Blake, Mistress of Girton College, was proposed and seconded and in the absence of any other candidate, was duly appointed. The parents, too, were called together by the Headmistress to choose a Lady Governor and Miss Milligan was appointed. So the Governing Body was widened and its contact with the school (and the other Trust schools) deepened.

Governors' response to war-time needs

It is interesting to note during the harsh years of war how the Governors responded to the needs of the time. Their consent for the award of leaving exhibitions is recorded annually; they accept Miss Dolby's recommendations of girls allowed to stay at school until they were 18; E. Lilley and W. Thornton in October 1914, Eunice Baxter, Frances Cobb, Myrtle Forrest, Kathleen Gambriel, Sarah Gaskin, Hettie Fuller, May Pearson and Ada Wesley in December, R. Scotchbrook, E. Wilson, G. Thornton, Winifred Odell, May Davison, Maud Hulatt, Dallas Burt-White, Phyllis Penn, Dorothy Buckley, Margaret Tresize and Gertrude Harrison in 1915; eleven girls in 1916, seven in 1917 and twelve in 1918. Term dates and holidays are fixed by them annually, visitors are appointed, both for the schools and the Boarding Houses. The Surveyor is instructed to deal with necessary upkeep to buildings.

The routine of dealing with examinations, the all important salary grants and grants for equipment, the remission of fees for girls who have been ill or the refusal of a place to a girl who did not qualify for residential reasons is interrupted by instructions in 1914 that 'the Headmistresses of the High and Modern Schools be authorised, in consultation with the Chairman of the Governors of the Girls' Schools, to allow as many daughters of Belgian refugees to attend classes at those schools without fee as they can provide instruction for with their existing arrangements. That in the cases of present pupils in the High and

Modern Schools for girls whose fathers have lost their lives in the war, the fees payable from 1st January 1915 may be the minimum prescribed.' (This was £4 p.a.) By March 1915 this concession was to be extended to applicants whose fathers had been incapacitated in the war. Occasionally girls were allowed to continue to attend while living with guardians other than their parents.

Another development of these years is the appearance of grants to members of staff who undertake vacation courses. In 1915 Miss Martin received £5 to attend a course for Women Teachers of Physics at Cambridge. Two years later Miss Hensman attended a similar course.

The rise in the cost of living led to a series of increases in staff salaries, and letters of thanks on behalf of the Staff were duly written by Miss Buckley. By 1919 Miss Dolby had submitted (and the Governors approved) a salary scale from £150 by £10 to £300 for graduates and £130 by £10 to £250 for non-graduates.

The increase in the number of boarders forced Miss Dolby to move from 8 Landsdowne Road to 47 Shakespeare Road, where she was allowed to take 25 boarders in 1917 and in the following year the boarding fee rose to £50 p.a. but by the end of 1918 Miss Dolby was planning to retire from the boarding house.

In all, with their financial responsibilities, their constant involvement in the maintenance of buildings, the acquisition of East Lodge, renting of the school field, granting of exhibitions and bursaries, the Governors were continuously and actively concerned with the running of the school. Their relations with Miss Dolby were cordial and correct. They obviously relied on her judgment and items such as 'That the Headmistress of the Modern School be empowered to make the best arrangements she can for the supply of stationery to the pupils for the ensuing school year', and 'That the action of the Headmistress of the Modern School in continuing to provide boarding accommodation for five day scholars . . . be approved and adopted' revealed their trust in a woman of long experience. After all, she had been Headmistress for twenty years when the war broke out, and it had been a period of almost uninterrupted progress – they had good reason to trust her.

The War ends

Writing her Christmas letter for the Old Girls' Association leaflet in 1918 Miss Dolby expressed her aims again, in the fullness of her experience. 'At so short a distance we cannot grasp the stupendous changes taking place in every direction, religious, political, social, economic and educational, not alone in our country, but all through the civilised world . . . The spirit of the times seems to call not for rest after the long struggle, but rather for greater endeavour, for higher ideals in every phase of life, for wider knowledge, clearer judgment and more definite aim than has been the case in the past.

'The idea of reconstruction dominates all minds; old beliefs, laws and social conventions are being cast aside, and out of the chaos a new order must be evolved. The ever-recurring problem is once again presented to us – that of discriminating between what is essentially vital, living and of permanent value in the old and that which is merely the accretion of time, of only transient worth, now outworn and become a stumbling block to the present generation; then having selected and adapted to the needs of our day that which the experience of ages has tested and found good, we must endeavour to graft upon the ancient stem those new spiritual, moral and social ideas which seem to promise the most perfect fruition. Here, then, is a task which calls for intellectual and moral truths, clear judgment, wide tolerance, generous openness of mind, and above all, wide, far-reaching vision. Truly our hearts might fail us in the welter of conflicting views and opinions were it not for the immense hope and radiant faith in the future, which is one of the most striking and uplifting characteristics of today.'

Before the next year was out, the first facile optimism born of the silence when the guns ceased, was over. The cruel impact of the influenza epidemic, the rising unemployment which resulted from hasty demobilisation, the revival of labour troubles which had been with such difficulty suppressed during the war, had all begun to erode men's faith and hopes. For women, some of the gains and most of the changes were irrevocable. The granting of women's suffrage (if only at the age of thirty), the fact that women had invaded many male preserves of employment, the numbers of widows and fatherless children left by the million high death toll of the trenches, had altered things for ever. In future, daughters as well as sons would become wage earners in offices, shops and factories to a far greater degree than ever before, and far fewer girls would go into domestic service.

Peace day was celebrated in Bedford on 3rd July 1919 with all the schools participating in the singing of suitable songs and hymns under the baton of Dr Harding. The new boundaries were drawn on European and world maps; the school closed down its War Savings Association, having collected a grand total of £573 10s 8d, but the girls and staff still contributed their pennies for Mrs Hockliffe's Tea for Disabled Soldiers, and sent a cheque for £18 for the 'Starving children of Europe'.

Girl Guide Companies founded

From the point of view of the girls, perhaps the most exciting event of the year was the formation of the school Guide Companies. The move was initiated after an address by Mrs Josselyn in January, and the company founded by Miss Grattan and Miss Whittington, who remained in charge for many years. By the summer a second company was formed and the two vied with each other. From the beginning, girls went to camp – first at Old Warden, then at Meppershall. In 1920 an entertainment was given at the Town Hall, and the profits used to buy the Company Colours and set up a camp fund. In the summer of 1921 they attended a County Rally at the High School field, at which the Chief Guide, Lady Baden Powell, was present. Their prowess was rewarded; the 1st Company won the County Challenge Shield for the year, the 2nd Company came third. In 1922 Miss Carter began her long association with the company, and in the next year both companies did well in the Eisteddfod Song Competition and the 2nd Company won the County Shield. It had been hoped when the companies were founded that they would train leaders for the future, and by 1923 Violet Goodman had become Lieutenant to the 14th Bedford Company and Gladys Horsford, Acting Lieutenant, at Dean.

Progress was maintained, with an average of 30 Guides in each company; song competitions, church parades and camp continued. In 1924 they went further afield, to Foxlease Park, which gave the opportunity for a visit to Beaulieu Abbey. The

'Cadet Corps' of Old Girls gave valuable assistance, both on Parade Nights and in camp.

In 1921 the numbers of the school reached a peak of 522, never again to be achieved until the Second World War. The III Upper and IV Lower forms were in four divisions, others in two, except for the top and bottom where there was only one form in each age group, so we get a picture of a school with an 11+ to 13+ age range much larger than the rest, and realise that many did not reach the V form and the public examinations.

Expansion

The numbers taking the Cambridge Senior Local Examinations increased; 28 out of 29 passed in 1919, 18 out of 19 in 1920, 28 in 1921 – with one Higher School Certificate – gained by Eva Dickens.

Memories 1921

Eva has cherished to the present day a photograph of the staff in 1921, many of whom had been there throughout her school life. 'First and foremost, of course', she writes, 'was Miss Dolby, our headmistress, sailing majestically into prayers, which at that period were held in the gymnasium. There were no chairs, so we stood in rather crowded rows with our school bags at our feet, in perfect order and in complete silence. Miss Buckley played for the hymn and while we filed out – most often a movement from a Beethoven piano sonata... Miss Dolby was very firm yet extremely kind and patient so that the Maths. lesson alone with her in her room in my last year did not at all alarm me. A great Headmistress!

'I have vivid memories of Miss Buckley reading from *Twelfth Night* and throwing herself so dramatically into the part of Sir Toby Belch that I feared she might actually drink from the pot of red ink she was brandishing. Miss Coltman's voice I remember so well, rather slow and cool, cutting down Lydia Bennet to size. She it was who lent us books for the summer holidays – *Idylls of the King* and *The Makers of Florence*, and did much to foster my love of literature, introducing me to Thackeray's novels and to much else...

'Beautiful Miss Alderson Smith taught Latin and we were all desolated when she left . . . Miss Crump, Miss Whittington and

Miss Grattan we (Sixth formers) met only at Games, and Gymnastics was taught by visiting staff from the P.T. College in Landsdowne Road. Miss Cranmer arrived at school when I was in the VI form and I remember being nervous at the prospect of a whole hour alone with her reading Marivaux and Molière. I need not have been worried – I soon looked forward to Tuesday afternoons.'

The list did not include one much loved mistress, Clara Porter, who had joined the staff in 1892 and taken over responsibility for the Lower School at East Lodge in 1918. She was away all the Summer term 1919 and died in August that year. She had devoted herself unsparingly to her girls, both the juniors and the seniors whom she took for games, and was remembered by all with great affection.

East Lodge

The younger girls started school in the lovely riverside surroundings of East Lodge. Margaret Litchfield (1921–27) writes, 'When in II Middle (Form Mistress, Miss Hilda Johnston) we occupied a large room on the ground floor with a huge window, the height and width of the room, looking out on to the gardens, which in those days stretched down to the river, and we played rounders in what is now part of the public riverside walk. We also acted *A Midsummer Night's Dream* in the gardens, although I cannot remember taking much part in the acting . . . It really was a most happy time spent in such pleasant surroundings.'

Audrey Coxan remembers, 'one form was in the former drawing room. I was fascinated to see the walls covered in wallpaper and a dado at least a foot deep, a riot of roses. For Assembly we went upstairs and through a bathroom that had an enormous bath . . . painted to represent marble. Once we were sent home because the river was rising rapidly and when we returned the cloakroom, formerly the kitchen, was in a sorry state and shoes left in pigeon-holes not wearable.'

Not all the time was devoted to work. Audrey continues, 'My first school hat was a very large brimmed boater with a navy and light blue zig-zag band, known to some as "thunder and lightning". The hat was a wonderful piece of sports equipment; a peg was driven into the grass in the lower garden at East Lodge, and the hat skimmed on to the peg.'

What did those happy eleven-year-olds learn in their idyllic school? A report of the period lists the subjects taken: Dictation, English Grammar and Language, History, Reading, Recitation, Geography, Natural History, French, Arithmetic, Scripture, Writing, Drawing, Brushwork and Needlework. The bulk of the work was in the hands of the form mistress, Miss Johnston, who had only just joined the staff. She was an Old Girl of the school and had trained at Stockwell Training College, London.

The following year, with Miss Grattan, their new form mistress, they were photographed in the garden; thirty of them in rather unbecoming, unadorned, pleated gym tunics, worn with a rather mixed selection of Peter Pan collared blouses. Nearly all have bobbed hair, parted at the side and fastened by a slide. The trees behind them form the same unspoilt background as has graced so many school photographs since.

The Kindergarten College (later Froebel College) sent students to help, particularly with Brushwork, Handwork and Geography throughout the year. This was one way in which Miss Dolby coped with the sudden and rather brief increase in numbers, which in January 1918 had been 333, in September 426, in September 1919, 468, September 1920, 516, September 1921, 522 and then the decline almost as rapid to 341 in 1926. Such changes meant the employment of a number of staff for short periods only, and in four years nearly thirty teachers joined the staff, many of them for a term or less, but a few like Miss Cranmer and Miss Carter to remain and add a major contribution to the life of the school.

Other changes

The playing field, too, was enlarged, the Pavilion moved and water laid on so that entertaining visiting teams became much easier. School activities flourished; at the 1921 Eisteddfod several girls won prizes, and a class choir and the Guides gained second places. A tremendous effort was made to help the Boys' Modern School raise funds for a new boathouse. The girls raised £60 by their Christmas present stall at the Bazaar, and added to the entertainment by putting on a dancing display. The Old Girls held winter meetings at school, and summer reunions at East Lodge, where games and competitions could take place in the garden. Higher Certificate and Senior Local Examinations occupied the Upper School, over 250 girls took R.D.S. examinations, with excellent results; the London Institute Needlework tests were also taken.

In September 1921, Miss Dolby first mentions the existence of prefects, when they are detailed to see girls out of downstairs dressing rooms at 1 p.m. and the following year she records B. Storr as Head of School and D. Hubbard, M. Calthorpe, D. Fletcher, K. Wooding and R. Webb as prefects. It is clear that the principle of training the older girls in responsibility and authority has been accepted, and that the growth in numbers has made this development more formal. An established VI form acts as a nursery for these young officials of the school.

The School Concert and distribution of certificates which had had to be held in the afternoon and the evening to accommodate the numbers of girls and parents, was now moved to the Corn Exchange, where the choirs could be seated on the platform lent by the Musical Society. A widely varied musical programme preceded and followed the distribution of certificates but we have no records of speeches or reports being made. As the school still had no proper hall, plays were often performed in the Boys' Modern School Hall, as when the staff produced *Aunt Grundy* for the O.G.A. in 1922 and then repeated it at the B.M.S. in aid of 'The Children's Country Holiday Fund' for which a collection raised over £13.

While the continuing business of organising the ever changing school, and making the best use of her fluctuating staff must have occupied most of Miss Dolby's time and thought, she remained deeply responsive to the best that was happening around her. Old Girls returning to school noted new and less formal teaching methods and old buildings were adapted to new purposes. In 1922, the old Rifle Range was connected to the South Block by a covered passage and part turned into a large, well-fitted new cloakroom. This set free another room for a Reference Library for forms V and VI, and the O.G.A. helped to fill the empty shelves, as did specific grants from the Trust. Next came a proper Assembly Hall, adapted from the Rifle Range, large enough to accommodate the whole school. The decline in numbers (linked perhaps to the growing economic problems of the day) made it possible to re-unite the school and so East Lodge was given up once more and the 'little girls' came back to the august surroundings of the 'Big School' in 1924.

The great idealistic movement of the day was the League of Nations and Miss Dolby arranged for lectures, and prizes were offered for the best essays on the subject. In her letter to the Old Girls for Christmas 1923, she urges them all to find out about and, if possible, join the League of Nations Union. Fully aware of its fragility, she saw no other way open to bring order into a troubled world. She noted also the important part played by women in its councils and urged her readers to play their part. The new Assembly Hall made it possible to bring together the Senior School for lectures and six of the Staff gave talks on the Empire after school on Friday afternoons; other lectures covered missionary themes, Dr Barnardo's, The Orchestra, Form in Music, the United States Exhibits in the B.M.S. Museum, Women and Girls in Ceylon. Many of these were illustrated by lantern slides.

Miss Dolby's retirement

At this time, Miss Dolby was over sixty, and her illness in January 1925 made it clear that she could not long continue. She retired at the end of the Christmas term, after an Open Day and School Concert at the Corn Exchange, followed by tea for sixty at the school, the Old Girls' Reunion and parties for the Upper and Lower School. An age had ended. She had been Headmistress for thirty-one years and had virtually created the school. She was universally beloved, and many Old Girls have written in her praise. 'As a new girl I thought she was very beautiful with her crinkly, silver-grey hair,' wrote Mary Wilkinson. 'Miss Dolby, what a wonderful Head!' says Winifred Valentine (*née* Finch). Staff and girls alike dreaded the change which was imminent but were reassured when they met her successor, Miss Tonkin, in the course of the Autumn term.

Miss Dolby's contribution to the school is inestimable. She took it over at a time of decline, steered it through three reigns and two wars, raised its academic standards, obtained leave for the girls to stay on to 18 so that they could go direct to the universities, greatly increased and improved its buildings. Above all, she had won the confidence of Governors, staff, girls and parents by her kindness, honesty and grace. Her records are as neat and factual in 1925 as they were in 1895. From before the Diamond Jubilee to the flapper age and the eve of the General Strike, she had upheld standards without allowing them to ossify into mere formalism. She had moved with the times, introducing uniform, Guides, dancing classes, but had not been a slave to fashion. Few schools have been better served and those who still remember her are well aware of it.

Music

Before we leave these foundation years of the school's life, let us remember, with those who were there, some of their continuing pleasures. The school was always deeply involved in music and drama. Miss Buckley, herself no mean musician, wrote in 1932, 'In my first term (1897) we had great fun rehearsing Haydn's *Toy Symphony* for the concert. The air resounded with the most discordant and unusual sounds. It seemed for some time unlikely that we should ever be able to adjust the pitch of piano and trumpet, the obstreperous Nightingale sought to eclipse the Cuckoo, and both had to be chastened and subdued. There were moments of black despair, but in the end we achieved almost a finished semblance of harmony.'

Year by year the Speech Day celebrations gave scope for music, and the programmes bring to us the flavour of these past occasions. The chosen songs include *Tit-Willow*, Sullivan, *Land of Hope and Glory* (chosen in 1905), *Golden Slumbers*, *Ye spotted snakes*, *The Sandman* to music by Brahms, *It was a lover and his lass*, Hilaire Belloc's *Cautionary Tales*, *Oh Sweet Content*, *The Manx Spinning Wheel Song*, songs from Ben Jonson's *Pan's Anniversary*, to music by Geoffrey Shaw, played by the orchestra. The range is extensive, the choice varied and robust. For years the school produced three choirs and their training was in the hands of Miss Huntington (of the Froebel College, Bedford) and Miss Buckley. This was the age of choirs dressed in white for concerts, with black stockings and shoes, but if the dress was of its period, the teaching was sensitive and progressive.

Two little anecdotes suggest the happy relationships and lifelong appreciation which resulted. Bessie Bryant (*née* Bates) recalls, 'One singing lesson, a caterpillar was crawling up my shoulder and I dreaded anything creepy-crawly and dared not touch it. Along came Miss Huntington, gave one look, and with her baton immediately knocked it off. I was never so grateful in my life.' Mary Wilkinson says, 'Music lessons with Miss Huntington were a joy to me; she was before her time in teaching us to breathe correctly. She even had one flat on the floor to test the depth of breathing!'

Instrumental music, too, was encouraged. In 1908, Dorothy Ehrhardt was the first recorded solo pianist at a school concert, and was greatly admired by the *Bedfordshire Times*' reporter of the day. The first violin solo came in 1912 when Ethel Staniford performed a Saltarella by Hans Sitt. Later we find singing Quartets and a Quintet and Trios, depending on the talent available from time to time. It appears that the girls were private pupils chiefly of Dr Harding and Mr A. de Reyghere, and many of them went on to take up music as a career.

One of these, Minnie Coward (*née* Mastin), tells us, 'One thrilling memory I have. After I went up to London for singing lessons and was singing professionally, I sang at one of the Old Girls' Reunions (1920) and I got a most warm welcome and ovation. Miss Buckley, on behalf of the Staff and Old Girls, welcomed me and said they were proud of me and my singing successes.'

Others included Phyllis Horton, Maud Freeman, Florence Willmer, Dorothy Marshall, all of whom reached professional standards, and Hilda Howe, whose lovely voice was often heard at school concerts and whose musical talent served the school in so many ways during her long association with it as a pupil and English teacher.

The continuous involvement of staff, pupils, choirs, instrumentalists and Guide Companies in the Bedford Eisteddfod from the earliest days is evidence not only of interest but also of excellence. Every year saw a crop of gold medals, cups and certificates in every available class. In 1923, Miss Dolby records:
Gold Medal awarded to:

A. Mathers	Solo singing
K. Stuart P. Pratt	Piano duet

L. Timmins	Piano
M. Freeman	Violin solos (2)
M. Williams	Elocution
I. Ibbott	Violin solo

The list can be paralleled year by year. In 1924, form singing competitions were started and an afternoon in the busy Summer term set aside for them and parents invited to hear the classes.

Drama

While it was possible to hold the annual School Concert at the Town Hall, dramatic interludes always formed a part of the entertainment. At first these were usually short French or German dialogues, one act plays or excerpts from classical plays, such as the scene from Schiller's *Wilhelm Tell*, produced in 1899. Later, English entertainment began with scenes from *Alice in Wonderland* in 1907, and later offerings were 'A Scene from *The Mill on the Floss*', and Hoffman's *Cautionary Tales* in 1910. The most ambitious of these plays, designed for the Corn Exchange and one long remembered by its participants, was a three act allegory called *Tomorrow*, by Kitty Barne which was produced in 1913 and repeated in 1916. 'The immense success of this was due partly to the real charm of the play, but more especially to the unusual organising ability of the Stage Manager, Miss Alderson Smith, the charming dances arranged by Miss Hadley, who gave her time most generously, and to the taste and ingenuity with which the costumes were devised. The play required a long list of quaint characters, and it was a pageant of beautiful colouring, with amusing dialogue, pretty songs, dances and tableaux, connected by a slender but charming story,' wrote Miss Buckley, who was involved with all this and many more dramatic activities.

Not until 1924 did the school possess its own Assembly Hall, and this severely limited the range of plays which could be tackled, though the boarders had produced *The Pirate of Ranora* and *The Don of Aquadulce*, both musical burlesques, during the war years. In consequence, the young amateur actresses did not have the opportunity of working at a full length play, but there is no doubt that they greatly enjoyed the many light-hearted pantomimes, pageants and sets of tableaux, with words written or adapted by the staff, which were a usual feature of parties and celebrations.

This emphasis on the musical and dramatic side of school work did not preclude an equal interest in games and gymnastics, where competitions and matches proliferated. Girls took part in hockey, tennis and rounders with form matches and individual cups to compete for and senior and junior gymnastic competitions occurred every year. These involved an assessment of classwork throughout the year as well as the actual display. Silver and bronze shields were awarded and the rooms must have been well decked with the rewards of the form's prowess. Swimming, too, had long been competitive though sometimes, as in 1924, bad weather prevented the holding of the sports.

Memories

This period of the school's history may well be closed by quoting some memories of Old Girls. Hilda Long (*née* Howe) writes, 'It was in the ground floor classroom overlooking St. Paul's Square that I met my doom one day in 1914. The lower part of the windows could only be opened by hand and even then one had to stand on the desks beneath to reach them. On this particular hot day, this had been done before we went out to Break and two minutes before the school trooped into the building again Miss Coltman asked me to shut them. In I went, mounted the desk beneath the first window and was enthralled to see part of the 51st Highland Division, then stationed in Bedford, rounding the Church on a route march. I waved to them, they waved back and whistled and more of this went on till I became aware of a deathly silence behind me. There stood Miss Coltman at her desk and the rest of the form motionless by theirs. Miss Coltman spoke, "Hilda, go to the VI form and ask Miss Buckley if you may sit at the back of the room for the rest of the morning!" How many girls throughout the school's history have been similarly caught out, and as efficiently handled!'

Joan Pearson (*née* Clark) recalls, 'There was a General Election and at lunchtime some of us girls were waiting at the Shire Hall to hear the result, the school then being in St. Paul's Square. Suddenly we heard a bell and everybody cheered. They thought the result was to be announced but it was Miss Buckley at the gate, ringing the bell. So one girl said, "We had better go in or old Buckets will be after us". A voice said, "Yes, Jessie, old Buckets will be after you," and she was standing just behind us.'

Ordinary girls, doing ordinary things, with a natural and reasonable attitude to staff and affairs; a staff, willing and able to give them the best of education and culture; pranks and high spirits, as from the group who christened themselves 'The Devil's Own Light Infantry' but never did anything mean or underhand. No wonder that in our oldest living Old Girl's words, 'It was a happy school.'

Quiet Progress 1925–1937

Miss Tonkin

It was natural that the announcement of Miss Dolby's forthcoming retirement should bring anxiety to both girls and staff; none of them could remember any other Headmistress; she was popular and the school was comfortable with her; it seemed unlikely that her successor would fit easily into her place. They were wrong.

Beatrice Alice Tonkin was forty-two years old when she took up her office. She had been educated privately and at East Putney High School, had read Modern Languages at Girton, obtaining 1st Class Honours in French and German in 1906. After two years teaching in Newport, she had obtained the London Teacher's Diploma, and had then taught at Fulham County Secondary School and at Abbeydale Secondary School, in Sheffield, until her appointment by the Harpur Trust.

From the beginning, Miss Tonkin impressed girls, staff and parents by her quick understanding of their problems and her patience in dealing with them. She had an appreciation of the deeper, spiritual forces and ideals which create the character not only of individuals but also of institutions. She soon became a much loved headmistress.

No drastic changes followed her appointment; but perhaps the Lecture-Demonstration in the Hall on the use of the Gramophone by Messrs Frazer suggested her realisation of the value of this aid to teaching. In her first term, too, the school orchestra was formally started under Miss Howe's baton, with Miss Carter leading the first violins and Miss Buckley the seconds. It was typical of the happy way in which the girls and staff always combine their musical talents. In the summer of 1926, the Class Singing Competition was augmented by a Folk Song Class for

Laying the foundation stone of the Milne building, 1937, see page 74.

Official opening of the Douglas Gordon building, 1967.

The Headmistress and Staff in 1958.

Distribution of A. level certificates, 1978.
Far left: Sir John Howard. Presenting award: Mr Brian Kemball-Cook.
Far right: Miss S. M. Morse, Headmistress.

The Douglas Gordon building, 1977.

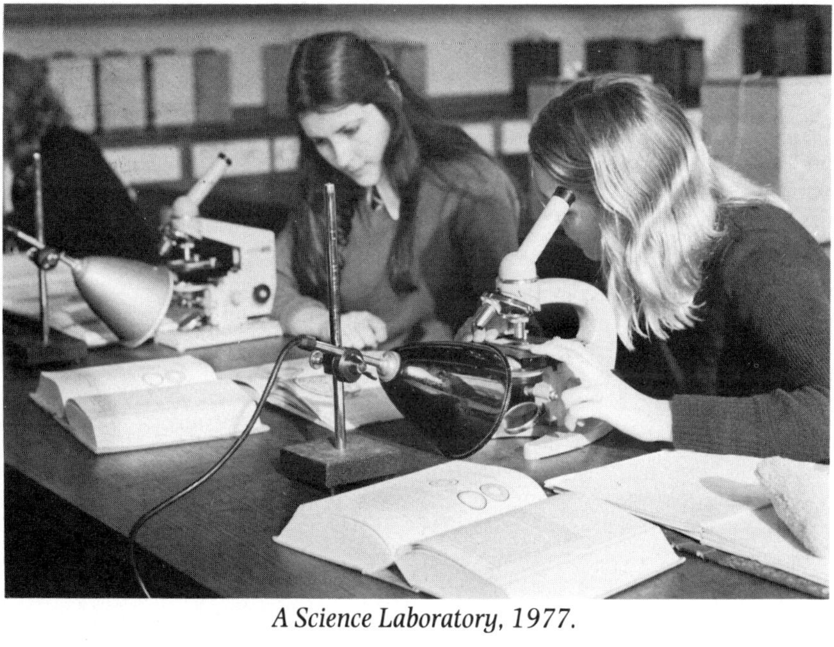

A Science Laboratory, 1977.

A Home Economics class, 1977.

The Lawson-Brown Swimming Pool, 1977.

Miss H. Lawson-Brown,
Headmistress 1955–70.

Miss S. M. Morse,
Headmistress 1970 to present day.

The Headmistress and Staff in 1982.

Aerial view of the school, 1982.

Modern Languages in the Mini-lab, 1982.

The Computer Room, 1982.

VI 2, 1981–82.

Miss Todman and Prep III 8, 1981–82.

which Miss Huntington presented a Silver Rose Bowl; parents were invited both to this and to the gymnastic competition. At the end of the school year the VI form presented *The Knight of the Burning Pestle* and gave the £4 5s 11d collected to the Games Fund. The V forms sat for the usual School Certificate Examinations; there were no candidates for the Higher Certificate. The Swimming and Tennis Cups were awarded as usual. A Sketching Club competition was held and three prizes gained. Neither the School Log nor the Old Girls' record of events makes any reference to the General Strike of that summer or to the increasing economic problems of the country. Rightly, the school kept its eyes fixed on its own goal, knowing that the gift of education which it offered to so many girls was increasingly important as the surrounding skies darkened.

Back to East Lodge

As the operation of the Direct Grant scheme developed, more and more girls came in by train from the country districts, often cycling to some small station like Flitwick to catch their trains into town. For them the school day started early and ended late. The school had little to offer in the way of space or comfort during the dinner hours, when all local girls and the boarders went home. When afternoon lessons became a regular feature of the timetable it became desirable to provide more adequately for the country girls. Miss Buckley took the new headmistress to see East Lodge, which was no longer being used for the Lower School, and Miss Tonkin conceived the idea of using the property as a centre for country girls. The Governors were persuaded to buy the building which they had previously leased from the Barnards, the local banking family. Basic equipment was provided, but to make it comfortable a Garden Fête was held on 20th July 1927. The parents of the country girls provided a special Country Produce Stall, and everyone worked with great enthusiasm. How it rained that day, but determination had its reward and £210 was raised to furnish the house. Hot dinners were provided, cooked by Mrs Pope, the caretaker's wife, and after dinner the girls had the choice between going into the garden to play or into the Recreation Room which was furnished with the proceeds of the Fête.

Cookery

Next came the equipping of a Cookery Room, of which Miss Carter, who taught in it from the beginning, writes, 'What a kitchen it was too! Designed of course by a man and I then had no say in the matter! The room was L-shaped; two sinks at one end, two stoves, one gas, one electric; and one solid fuel stove. The top of the latter was in sections to allow for expansion, and it also enabled black smoke to emerge when the wind was in the wrong direction. Often I had to do a hasty clean up before my form arrived. There was no refrigerator or proper food storage and the only place to keep such things as fats, meat, etc. was in a safe hanging on an outside wall. To get to this, one heaved up a heavy window and crawled out on to what was the roof of a bay window of the room below. I soon had this changed to a ventilated safe inside the room. In spite of all this, we coped – and indeed served a very good lunch for about thirty governors and wives at the time of the laying of the foundation stone of the present building.

Every Christmas we had an exhibition of Christmas cakes in the St. Paul's building – about seventy cakes, and this included those made by the staff, who had an evening class in my kitchen . . . Every girl had to carry her cake from Cardington Road to St. Paul's Square and all the traffic was held up for us.'

Alterations in St. Paul's Square

At the same time considerable alterations were in progress in the main buildings; two large windows were made in the Gymnasium to let in the sun and air from the river side and during the Christmas holidays the roof was provided with a ceiling of lath and plaster in place of the rough underside of the tiles. This not only improved the appearance of the hall, but also made it easier to heat. Next on the list was the provision of a new front door and vestibule with a flight of stone steps to the first floor to make access safer and easier. These alterations made possible the provision of a waiting room for parents and visitors; it was for this entrance hall that the O.G.A. presented the oak panelling and the honours board, which now adorn the present school entrance hall. It may amaze us, in these inflationary times, to note that the cost was £30! Miss Tonkin found some difficulty in setting a standard for inclusion on the honours board, but numbers and space made it essential to limit it to university degrees or their equivalent, and even so, the board was half full when erected. This dignified new entry was the last change in the old buildings in St. Paul's Square. The shape of things to come was already adumbrated by the ownership of Dame Alice House and the purchase of the land adjoining, which was developed as a playing field for use in September 1929. The official opening took place on 26th October, when a match was played against the Cedars, Leighton Buzzard. It was a joy to play on a pitch with a good surface, 'undisturbed by trains thundering past, and without fear of the encroaching builder', after all the years of rented fields.

As in the early years of the school, home had been the fundamental centre of a girl's life, so in these years it seems as though school become the focus of interest. It was the age of the schoolgirl story, and there was tremendous enthusiasm for and loyalty to the school. The gym. tunic had taken over as uniform wear for physical activities; uniform hats and blazers proudly proclaimed membership of a special society to the outside world. A sense of privilege was encouraged, and within the society of school, lesser groupings were developed to enable loyalty to be a more personal thing. At first it was the form, a centre for more than work, as form competition became the order of the day. Singing competitions, 'drill' competitions, hockey and netball form tournaments divided into Senior and Junior, swimming races, competitions for the tidiest form room, the lowest number of disorder marks, the greatest number of high term-average marks, were all keenly contested.

The House System

Form competitions had the major disadvantage of trying to compare the work and abilities of girls of widely differing ages, and even the division into Upper and Lower School could not really disguise the anomalies. This, and the need for units small enough for everyone to be known and to have a personal niche, led to the introduction of the House System. Miss Tonkin hesitated over this, since a House system is always somewhat artificial in a day school, and the number of boarders was never (nor indeed could it legally be) great enough to influence the composition and organisation of the school. At the beginning of the Summer term 1930, four houses were formed, named, predictably, after four women saints. Quite why St. Ursula, St. Etheldreda, St. Hilda and St. Bridget were chosen, we do not know, but the names were voted on by the girls in each form and house colours chosen, green, yellow, red and mauve respectively, to be worn as a bar shaped brooch, and special colours appointed for outstanding honours gained for the House. A captain and a committee of girls ran each House and the staff, both full and part-time, were allocated to them. The four captains wrote an introductory note for the *Uisage* and pointed out that the vertical division of the school would add zest to competition and that more girls would be able to gain places in House teams than could possibly represent the school. 'Above all,' they wrote, 'the House being so much greater a unit than the Form, the spirit which inspires one to work hard, behave well and play with all one's might to win credit for the House should be much keener and more powerful.'

The award of House Colours was to depend on marks allotted for excellent work, deportment, holiday competition, gaining colours or half colours in hockey, netball, rounders or tennis and in prowess at swimming. A House Cup was awarded on the total of points gained by members and registers were to be kept, showing the contributions of individuals towards the total. The first major House event was the Summer Sports Day, held on 3rd July from 4–6.30 p.m. on the field, with tea in Dame Alice House garden. Apart from the flat races, much of the programme consisted of comedy events – three-legged races, sum race, cycle, egg and spoon. The climax was the House relay, both Senior and Junior event being won by St. Hilda's.

The magazines reflect a lively interest in House affairs, and House parties and entertainments were frequent. In October, St. Ursula's held a Fancy Dress Carnival in aid of House funds, and included tableaux of the pilgrimage of St. Ursula and her martyrdom, the House Song, ballroom dancing, side shows and refreshment stalls. It was all very jolly and in the best 'schoolgirl' tradition. The House Song – a homespun affair, started somewhat warily:

'Princess of Cornwall, virgin of fame
Still through the ages we honour thy name
Lead us, brave Ursula, though not to Rome
But in the precepts and maxims of home'

but ended with enthusiasm:

'Ursula guides us, sing the great name,
Blazon it far on the swift wings of fame.'

House notes catalogue the successes of individuals and reveal the wholehearted support given by members of staff who masterminded tennis tournaments, crossword puzzle competitions and plays, which kept the girls happy and raised money for future activities.

The Society of the Open Mind

Another grouping much encouraged by the Staff was the 'Society of the Open Mind'. This was founded in June 1929 for the purpose of encouraging dramatics and debates. Meeting twice or three times a term, and averaging about 70 members, they debated the predictable topics, starting with school uniform; other meetings heard papers read by different form groups; Hobbies for IV Lower, Sport for IV Upper; Art for V and the English novel for VI. At other times the members went for conducted tours of the Post Office, to the Gas Works, to Barratt's shoe factory at Northampton. Still other meetings took the form of play readings; members of staff read *Arms and the Man*, to an appreciative audience, IV Upper acted *The Princess and the Woodcutter*. Staff plays, talks about holidays in Canada and U.S.A., visits to London to art exhibitions and to see plays such as *Clive of India* at Wyndham's Theatre, and to Whipsnade, Oxford and Cambridge – all were organised under the umbrella of the Society, whose membership and activities flourished in the thirties, affording a light-hearted glimpse into some of the cultural and industrial developments of the day. Until the Second World War disrupted the school, with problems of transport, accommodation of an evacuee school and the increasing restrictions of every kind, the Society flourished, but soon after it was painted in on the mural at the top of the stairs in the new building, its life was over.

Other long-term interests of this period were the League of Nations' Union, the Guide Companies – now expanded to three, making of 'guild' garments, given usually to Dr Barnardo's homes, but in times of need, to other groups, the building of St. Christopher's Church in Luton, financed mainly by children, the Bedford Eisteddfod or Musical Festival, the Missionary Society, and all of these were assisted and supported by the staff. Their popularity and the widely varying subjects discussed and places visited, suggest that the school was indeed a society of the Open Mind, alive to the affairs of the day as well as preparing girls for examination.

This social and political awareness is further seen in the response to the needs of a harsh and depressing period of national history. In 1931 Margaret Valentine and Joan Timmins were sent to the Junior Summer School at Geneva and spent a very happy week attending meetings, lectures and going on excursions in Switzerland. On their return they gave a lecture to the school explaining what they had learnt and experienced there. The Guild of Help arranged the 'adoption' of a school in the Rhondda Valley, and a sewing party was formed to make suitable garments and a collection of £3 was sent. Even the Jubilee Pageant was given three times in aid of the Unemployment Fund in 1932, and Ivy Mayhew and Eileen Dodd, dressed as Sir William Harpur and Dame Alice his wife, presented a cheque for £30 to Prince George at the Rotary Club's Elizabethan Fair, standing in the rain by the Market Cross, on this 'thrilling occasion'. 1936 saw the 'adoption' of a family at Eden Pit by some of the forms, and parcels of clothing were dispatched to the family, and later another needy household was sent cash for Easter fare, and clothing. Arrangements were even considered by which money could be deposited at a local shop for necessities.

In 1937, at Miss Tonkin's suggestion, the school contributed towards the maintenance of some 4,000 Spanish refugee children who were brought to England. A series of whist drives was organised by the senior forms and the £4 collected at the first two was sent to the Basque Relief Fund.

From the point of view of the school, the great events of the Thirties were the celebration of the Golden Jubilee and the planning and construction of a new school building.

The Golden Jubilee

First the Jubilee. Schools have a tendency to regard age as virtue and to celebrate accordingly, but B.G.M.S. had rather more reason to rejoice than have many others. After an uncertain start, it had achieved a position in the town; its Direct Grant status, with the increasing number of 'free place' scholars admitted, meant that it was creating a ladder of opportunity for girls of ability from the whole County area, and in so doing, surely serving to the full the purpose for which the original endowment had been made by Sir William Harpur. The celebration came at the beginning of the Summer term, 1932. First came a play by the O.G.A. – *The Lilies of the Field* – which was presented in the B.M.S. hall to parents and friends and afterwards to the school in their own hall. Then the first public event of the Jubilee; a Thanksgiving Service at St. Paul's Church on Saturday 30th April. A congregation of present pupils, Old Girls, staff, governors, parents and friends joined in gladly with the hymns and listened to Canon Woodward's address centering on the thought that it is 'the true work of the true school to train its members in those great foundational principles on which character is built. There are two fundamentals; self reverence and self-denial . . . If a school sends out into the world citizens imbued with these two characteristics . . . then surely such a school is in the truest and highest sense of the word a success'. In the evening the O.G.A. met for dinner in the Gymnasium and the ritual signing of menus, which kept both Miss Dolby and Miss Tonkin busy! Speeches, toasts and presentations made it a happy and exhilarating time – a climax for the O.G.A. of 21 years of life and one in which humour played a very large part.

On the Sunday afternoon, the Governors held a reception at school for some 200 Old Girls, and a display of form and staff photographs gave a great deal of pleasure. Some of the original pupils who had never been in the St. Paul's Square building, were able to be present, and to admire the displays of art and needlework which proved that the modern miss was not behind her forerunners in these gentle arts.

The week of celebration continued with two performances of the pageant of *Lessons through the Ages*. This series of episodes, arranged by different members of staff and linked by interludes of song and dance organised by Miss Huntington, Miss Stuart-Fox, Miss Freda Ginn and Miss Read, Miss Angus and Miss Hill of the P.T. College, was opened by a prologue in Shakespearian blank verse, written by Miss Cranmer and spoken by the Head Girl. The text of this work, illustrated with photographs of each episode, proceeded from a lively Stone Age scene to a carefully composed and authentically dressed tableau of the official opening of the school in 1882. It was issued as part of the term's activities, and the young actresses, poised and composed, smile back at us from its pages. The pageant ended with a procession of the entire school, from the youngest to the Headmistress, so that everyone, even if not in costume, was seen to be part of this great unfolding of educational progress.

The Parents' Association Dance on the following night, was enhanced by the re-enactment of the period dances from the pageant, which formed the most pleasing feature of a happy evening. When finally the Friday Sports afternoon was over, both staff and girls must have relaxed in great relief. It had all gone off very well indeed.

The High School, with which B.G.M.S. had once shared buildings, celebrated its Jubilee on the following week-end, with a comparable round of festivities.

Parents' Association founded

The mention of the Parents' Association leads to a consideration of the foundation of that organisation. The idea was mooted by Miss Tonkin at meetings in July 1928 that followed two Open Days, and in the following month a Provisional Committee was set up of some 15 fathers and 15 mothers, and the Association came into being on 1st November of that year. Its expressed objects were (and are) 'To foster and support the welfare of the B.G.M.S. by all legitimate means; to take such steps as may be necessary to advise members on careers and employment for their girls; to provide means for social fellowship amongst the members.' Each girl was given a letter and enrolment form for her parents. In pursuance of these objectives, a series of talks on careers for girls was started when Miss Tonkin, with three Old Girls, two of whom were teaching in Bedford and one who was in training at Homerton, gave a detailed account of the demands of the profession, not least of which, she insisted, were 'resilience, both of body and spirit, and a deep-rooted belief in the perfectibility of human nature'. A month later, it was the turn of the Local Government Service. For Shorthand-Typists salaries ranged from £40–£165 a year and there was a possibility of a woman rising to a semi-administrative post at £225 p.a. By the end of 1934, talks had been given on Nursing, 'The remuneration is not great, but it is secure. This vocation is not overcrowded and is safe from masculine invasion. It is a life of discipline, hard work and long hours – sometimes 13 per day. After the general training . . . a post as Staff Nurse may be obtained (salary £40 to £60) and later as Sister (Salary £70 p.a.).' The Civil Service and Post Office were also explained, and the advantages of regular holidays and security were extolled.

Soon a series of Summer Fêtes was instituted, both to amuse and entertain, and in June 1934 a concert party, clown, side-shows and dancing provided a happy, if wet, Thursday activity. By 1935 the objective of these fêtes had become the provision of hard tennis courts, then costing £125 each; a considerable sum to raise in those days. Old English 'Shoppes', an auction of autographed photographs of sport and film stars, teas, a Punch and Judy Show, all contributed to the profit of £30 made that 4th July, and the new tennis courts were duly opened on 2nd October 1937.

To Cardington Road

By 1937, a far greater scheme was in being. The buildings in St. Paul's Square, much loved as they were, were cramped and old. Miss Tonkin had long wanted to see the school established for the first time in buildings designed and equipped solely for it. The purchase of Dame Alice House and of the playing field alongside it provided an ample site. The situation was attractive, not too far from the centre of the town, between the river and Cardington Road. It had only one disadvantage, the river was slow moving and liable to flood. Many times in the early years, wiseacres were able to say, 'I told you so.'

The building was the result of co-operation between the town and county councils and the Harpur Trust. The architect, Oswald P. Milne, himself an Old Boy of Bedford School, was set quite a complex task by the determination of the Governors to keep Dame Alice House, link it with the main block, but set that block much further back from the road. The King's Ditch, the Anglo-Saxon fortification of southern Bedford, further complicated the situation. It is a measure of Mr Milne's success, that the building he designed still looks effective and attractive some forty years later.

Foundations laid

From the vantage point of her Cookery Room in Dame Alice House, Miss Carter watched every stage of the building and recorded it in photographs, splendidly mounted in a souvenir volume. On 11th February 1937 the measuring of the site began, and then the old cottage which occupied part of the site was taken down. By early March, work had begun in earnest and the foundations were dug. In May, Miss Tonkin ceremonially laid bricks, in the Hall, Chemistry Laboratory and main corridor. The building proceeded rapidly, in spite of early flood delays, and the official Laying of the Foundation Stone by Lady Luke of Pavenham took place on 24th June 1937. The Governors and principal guests were received in the Dame Alice House gardens before lunch, which had been prepared and was served by the cooks of V Remove and IV Upper B, who posed for their photographs on the front steps – wearing cotton dresses, frilled aprons and mob caps and the cornflowers of the school badge. The ceremony was under the chairmanship of General Sir Walter Braithwaite and was attended by representatives of town and county education authorities and the Mayor and Mayoress of Bedford. Passing through a Guard of Honour formed by the school Guides to the presentation of bouquets and the singing of Kipling's *Dedication* by the school, Lady Luke proceeded to place beneath the stone carefully chosen souvenirs of the day, and then with trowel and mallet tapped the lowered stone into place, wishing that 'the foundations of the characters of the many girls who pass through the new school will be as firm as this stone'. Blessed and eulogised by Mr G. C. Walker, the building was then left to the scurrying ranks of craftsmen and labourers, who, through the months that followed, continued to 'build it strong and straight, and true'.

The new buildings

The frontage of the building, with its exceptionally pleasing interplay of curves and strong horizontal lines, still virtually unchanged, shows how the requirements of the site evoked from the architect an original and wholly acceptable interpretation of the needs of the school in bricks and mortar. The curve of the cloakroom, arched over the King's Ditch, echoed by the semicircular entrance, with the splendid window of the staff common room over it, led into a crush hall defined by the main staircase partially encircling it, but beyond these enfolding curves lay the straight definitive lines of functional corridors. Only ten all-purpose classrooms were provided, each with green 'blackboard' and fibre-boarded space for pictures. The Hall and Library were plastered, with the lower part panelled in oak, to match the oak panelling which was the Old Girls' gift to the old building, and which was re-erected in the entrance hall, with the honours board. The interior brick finish must have seemed very modern and functional in 1938. Three Science Laboratories, Art and Craft rooms, Geography room, Lecture Room and Gymnasium completed the tally of teaching rooms, and an administrative corridor provided space for medical inspection room,

waiting room, secretary and headmistress.

The school was then basically a two stream Grammar School, with a preparatory department and a small, but vigorous VI form. The building was equipped for 360 girls, and that number seemed a likely average for some years to come. The great gifts of the new building were an ordered and spacious working area, and a wide level playing field on the site. Hard paved areas for recreation and netball, the already existing hard tennis courts contrasted with a glorious informal garden, and the varying bridges over the King's Ditch were complemented by the splendid beech and chestnut trees which dominated the enclosed parts of the grounds.

B.G.M.S. in Cardington Road 1938–1945

Term begins

On 14th September 1938 term began in the new building. On the platform at prayers were the Mayor (Mr Sowter), Messrs Lansberry, Neate, Osborne, Rickard, Sharman and Mrs Coleman with Mr Liddle (Headmaster of B.M.S.). The brief traditional service led by Miss Tonkin included the hymns *Praise, my soul, the King of Heaven* and *Father of Men*. After reading the class lists for the new school year, the Headmistress gave a brief address: 'Not quite fifteen months ago, on Midsummer Day 1937, the ceremony of Laying the Foundation Stone of this building took place. You will see the stone in the exterior wall of this hall, facing the playing field, below the eagle crest. When the stone was laid a small space was left behind it and in that space was laid a metal box containing rather a strange collection of small or rather small objects. There was the London newspaper, *The Times*, for 24th June, a copy of the Jubilee number of the school magazine, four house bars with house colours, stamps of the reign of George V and Edward VIII, as well as the coronation stamps of our present King and Queen: some silver and copper coins of the new reign, the programme of the Foundation Stone ceremony, and this little bundle of things was held together with the dark and light blue of our school colours.

'Now the sealing up of this little collection of things had and has a meaning for us, and that is why I am reminding you about it today. In the first place, this is not a new school. It is an old school – 56 years old – and it has a long and honourable tradition; it belongs to an old foundation stretching back into the past, and we remember with gratitude our founders, Sir William Harpur and Dame Alice, his wife – without whose charitable thought this school would not have come into being.

'The Jubilee magazine stands for loyalty to all that is good in our traditions (and it is a great joy to have with us today so many Old Girls and past mistresses who have helped to build up those traditions).

'The house bars stand for comradeship – to remind us that we are members one of another and that when any member suffers others suffer, and when any member rejoices, the others rejoice too.

'The stamps and the coins signify our desire to be true and faithful servants of the Commonwealth, good citizens doing an honest day's work, and not only so, but coming 'ardent to the daily task', as our motto says.

'On the programme were the words of the hymns which expressed the sense of our dependence upon God for all the blessings of this life.

'These things, then, are built literally into the fabric of the school, and it is my great hope and desire that these things, faith, hope, love, loyalty, together with that lesser but still important grace, courtesy, may be the watchwords of our daily life together here in this beautiful building which our architect, Mr Milne designed and which our builders, Messrs Foster of Kempston, have built with such speed and skill and careful attention to detail, and which the hands of so many men have laboured to beautify.

'Each of us, young and old alike, has a part to play in making this school a true temple of learning, in which the only rule is "Be happy; add but the other grace, Be good." '

So they led out to start the day's work; the surroundings new, but the desks and books and equipment mainly that which had been brought from the old building. There was a flurry of parties: to 'warm' the Staff Room and congratulate Miss Knight on twenty-one years' service; to thank the workmen and cleaners for their share in the success of the venture; the House-warmings; an 'At Home' for parents, with a chance to inspect the building and finally, in December, the formal opening by Sir William Marris, KCSI, KCIE. Sir William had had a long and distinguished career in the Imperial Service and had recently been Vice-Chancellor of Durham University, and spoke somewhat sombrely – as well he might in December 1938 – of the need to put the welfare of others first, as a step towards ridding the world of suspicion, tension, greed and danger. Lady Marris presented the certificates; seven at Subsidiary Standard, Higher School Certificate and twenty-five at School Certificate level. Then Miss Buckley presented a portrait of Miss Dolby, who was, happily, present at that occasion. Many other gifts to the new school were announced and the meeting was wound up with votes of thanks in which the Mayor, Mr Braggins, extolled the happy co-operation between Borough Council, County Council and the Governors of the Harpur Trust.

Gifts helped to beautify the clean-cut lines of the new buildings; the table and chair for the Hall from the O.G.A.; the lectern from B.M.S. and the vases in the entrance hall from the Parents' Association, a rose bed, money for plants, etc.

In January the school received another gift. The Suffrage Society for Bedford, which had fought before the First World War for Votes for Women, presented their orange and black banner, striped like a rising sun, and from the back of the Hall Gallery for thirty years or more it looked down on the young, who accepted as natural that emancipation for which the struggle had been so harsh and so long.

The first flood

Helped by the enthusiasm of some of the girls, the gardens were planned and dug and planted, but there was a great deal of worry when in January 1939, the river rose, and the school was surrounded by flood water. The central heating boilers were affected and on 30th January the school was closed for the day, an event which called forth at least one scornful letter in the *Bedfordshire Times*. 'Sir, the new Bedford Girls' Modern School is unable this morning, owing to floods, to accommodate its scholars, as everyone outside the Town Council and the Harpur Trust [*sic*] knew that it must be sooner or later . . .'. Indeed the situation on the flat flood plain of the river meant that the school would always be in danger unless the flow of the Ouse were skilfully managed, and the new buildings of the 1960s werc deliberately raised to avoid a repetition of the embarrassing floods of the early years on the site.

The impact of this mishap was slight, and the Spring term of

1939 saw the usual series of lectures, outings, matches, the O.G.A. reunion and a joint O.G.A.-P.A. dance. The press photograph shows the dancers, ladies in long full-skirted dresses, modestly cut, and many with tiny puff sleeves, men in dinner jackets. It was 7th March 1939 and the world they knew was already crumbling around them. Munich was a bad joke of the past; National Service had begun; gas masks were being prepared for the civilian population. A week after the happy dance at B.G.M.S. Nazi troops entered Prague, and the state of Czechoslovakia was dismantled and absorbed by Germany and Hungary. The whole Nazi apparatus of anti-Semitism, secret police and Storm Troopers moved in not only to German speaking Bohemia, but also to Slavonic lands beyond. Now Hitler proclaimed that he had no further demands – except Danzig, a free port, accessible through Poland and linking East Prussia to the Fatherland. At last the British Government and Daladier's France realised the danger of a German drive to the east and south-east, and a pledge was given to Poland – a pledge that was to involve all of Europe in a count-down to disaster.

Whatever the international situation, the routine of daily life must be continued; the Summer term 1939 started on 2nd May: almost immediately a series of A.R.P. lectures began, and practice with gas masks and a visit to a 'Gas-Chamber' (the words had not yet acquired their horrifying Nazi connotation) was arranged. A series of First Aid lectures was planned for July. On 13th and 14th June the staff presented three short plays, *The Spartan Girl*, *The Lift that Failed* and *Passion, Poison and Petrification*, in the school hall in aid of the Refugees' Fund and the Soroptimists' Good Cause. It was the first time the stage had been used with all the new lights and curtains. The staff, in spite of the Summer term rush of examinations and activities, made time to amuse their friends and were greatly admired by their pupils who were allowed to attend the dress rehearsal.

In June, King George VI and Queen Elizabeth visited Canada and the U.S.A. where they met President Roosevelt. Moved to tears by the welcome they had received, and psychologically buttressed by the immense popularity which had almost engulfed them, they returned to England on the liner *Empress of Halifax*. On 22nd June the school assembled to listen to a broadcast of their tumultuous welcome home. It was to be the last carefree broadcast for many a long day.

A 'Keep Fit' festival in Russell Park, the Society of the Open Mind outing to Kenilworth and the VI form performance of *Coriolanus*, and all the bustle of end of term lists and grades and examination marks covered up for the girls the heavy hearts of the adults as they absorbed their A.R.P. and First Aid lectures, and coped with more and more directives for the future. The age was drawing to a close and no one could foresee the future. One year only in the new building, to enjoy the space and light, the pleasant gardens and wide playing fields, the airy classrooms and purpose-built laboratories, the splendid gymnasium and quiet library. After all the years of difficulty, it was little enough.

The Second World War

The summer holidays gave little peace to Miss Tonkin, who was soon involved in plans for the accommodation of Woodford County High School, which was to be evacuated from London. When term began on 21st September 1939, the basic arrangements were already made. B.G.M.S. would have the building in the mornings, managing to get in six short periods daily and some Singing, Games and Art in the afternoons. Woodford County High School, which had fewer girls to accommodate, took the afternoon shift. Refuge rooms were arranged in the Science corridor, dining room and laundry, and windows were bricked up and stout partitions made to serve as Air Raid shelters. The black-out meant that all functions had to be kept to daylight hours, even though black curtains were hung at corridor windows and in many of the rooms.

As Miss Tonkin put it, writing to the O.G.A. in 1946, 'When I look back, the war years seem to have run together into one long blank period because, I suppose, we were keyed up to endure what had to be endured and closed our minds to the other things. Or perhaps it was just the mass of things that we had to carry in our minds which blunted the edge of our perception.'

Rationing, the need to use the Dining Room as a shelter, and the fact that, for the majority of girls, school ended at 12.30, meant that no hot lunches were served, though cocoa and coffee were available for those who brought cold lunches. Both work, games and charitable efforts continued as usual, though the objects of the latter changed, and we read of clothing made for the evacuees at 48 Cardington Road, and gifts for Finnish, Russian and Yugoslav refugees, according to the progress of the war.

Woodford County stayed for two years, their numbers declining steadily as parents recalled their children after the first months of 'phoney' war, and, by autumn 1941, only a handful of girls and two members of staff remained to be incorporated into B.G.M.S. If organised school evacuation came to an end, individual evacuation increased and in the five years of war, B.G.M.S. accepted girls from forty-nine other schools and the numbers in school rose from 360 to nearly 600 in September 1946. In face of such a development, every corner of the building had to be utilised and a jig-saw pattern of form movements organised. Shortage of books and paper, clothes rationing, the endless paperwork of bureaucratic administration, fire-watching by day and night, attempts to grow food on part of the school field, all helped to exhaust a devoted Headmistress and staff. 'I do not believe,' wrote Miss Tonkin, 'that anyone not immediately concerned with a school could realise the amount of writing which the fire-watching involved, or worse still, the issue of extra coupons to over-weight and over-size children. Lists and lists and more lists and then cards and cards and more cards.'

Games activities had to be cut, and matches could only be played with teams within walking or bicycling distance, so that the presence of Woodford for two years gave some outside matches and others were arranged with the Froebel College, the Central School, and Rye County School (evacuated).

Other activities continued on a muted level; house-warmings occupied an hour in the morning, plays and Speech Days had to be afternoon affairs. After three o'clock in winter, the cleaners had to scurry round, so only one afternoon lesson could be given, even when there was room enough for afternoon school to restart.

No heroic efforts were required of the school. The one term-time air raid took place just as the school assembled in the morning, and was not really noticed by everyone. There were many alerts and girls had to scurry to refuge rooms: Miss

Woodger had a lively story of a sewing class dashing across the lawn waving its white pyjama tops merrily as the planes flew overhead. In the refuge rooms, groups continued lessons in semi-darkness, French and Mathematics blending somewhat awkwardly with English and Sewing. Miss Pugh remembered four classes in the old 'science' corridor, she teaching Biology at one end and 'Hunty' conducting a singing class at the other. But no one was hurt and the buildings were unharmed. There was, indeed, much to be thankful for.

The Diamond Jubilee

The Diamond Jubilee was celebrated more quietly in this atmosphere. The article contributed to the *Bedfordshire Times* opened, 'To some it may be a matter of surprise that we are celebrating a Diamond Jubilee, for another ten years in the life of a school are not the equivalent of the next ten years in the life of a married couple who have had their golden wedding, or of a sovereign who has celebrated her Jubilee. That we are celebrating it in war-time may be a further matter of surprise, but it is this latter fact which provides the explanation. We are keeping our Diamond Jubilee just because the country is at war; firstly as an indication of our calm and sober confidence in the ultimate victory of a righteous cause; secondly because the past ten years have brought us much for which we are grateful; and finally because in view of the changes which will inevitably come we wish to re-dedicate ourselves to the service of God so that we may go on to the future with courage and hope renewed.' The school, Old Girls and friends joined in the Thanksgiving Service held at St. Paul's on 2nd May. The following afternoon the Headmistress and staff were 'At Home' to the Old Girls, while the second performance of the Staff play, *The Would-Be Nobleman*, concluded the celebrations the following Saturday.

After 1942, afternoon school was fully restored and dinners for the country girls resumed. At first, groups of fifty at a time went to the British Restaurant in Gwyn Street, but the last set were often late for afternoon school, so then, by the co-operation of Mr R. Turner of the Bedford Gas Company, the food from the British Restaurant was driven in containers down to school. Increasing numbers eventually made this impractical and once more the school kitchen served 'a good hot appetising meal' which the girls carried from the hatch to the table for themselves.

Music and Drama

The school's interest in music and the arts continued and, indeed, was fostered by the presence in Bedford of the B.B.C. Symphony Orchestra; on 31st January 1942 a concert was given, attended by the school, conducted by Clarence Raybould, of which the second part was broadcast; on 2nd June the school attended a Children's Concert at the Corn Exchange, which was conducted by Dr Malcolm Sargent. Joint carol concerts with B.M.S. at the Corn Exchange, in aid of Services' Charities, became the main annual Christmas festivities. At these carol concerts the school was privileged to have the assistance of some of the B.B.C. singers and instrumentalists as soloists, and Dr Thalben Ball was the organist. The tireless enthusiasm and hard work of Miss Huntington made these occasions a delight both to participants and audiences.

If music flourished, so did drama, both indigenous and imported. In 1940 the 'Pilgrim Players' presented *Tobias and the Angel* in the Hall; a few weeks later a school Nativity Play was performed. The newly formed elocution class produced scenes from *As you Like It* and *Romeo and Juliet* in the spring of 1942. In *The Would-Be Nobleman,* full use was made of the musical talents of Mrs Long (Hilda Howe) and Miss Carter, and the acting skill of Miss Lewis, Miss Kett and Miss Cranmer. Later that summer the VI form produced *The Admirable Crichton.* Six girls took part in a B.B.C. Nativity Play which was broadcast that year. In March 1943 the school gave an afternoon's entertainment in aid of the Mayor's fund for China. Mimes were enacted to passages from Pearl Buck's books, *Dragon Seed* and *The Good Earth.* The Junior Elocution class produced a play *The Stolen Prince* in the Chinese style and VI form girls recited translations of Chinese poems. By July, the Elocution pupils were able to produce *A Midsummer Night's Dream* – a performance which was much enjoyed. This time the proceeds were for the 'Save the Children Fund'. In 1944 the Ballet Rambert visited Bedford, and many of the school enjoyed this form of dance for the first time; perhaps this inspired the staff ballet which formed part of the variety performances of *Mixed Grill*, given again, in aid of the 'Save the Children Fund'. The last of the war time productions was a full scale presentation of *Twelfth Night*, in which the staff and girls were equally involved, the staff taking the comedy characters of the sub-plot, while the girls played the more straightforward romantic characters. Three performances this time, in aid of the fund for the Partisans of Yugoslavia, raised over £90, and earned the actresses a glowing report in the *Bedfordshire Times and Standard*.

To these major activities must be added the continuous round of semi-routine fund raising efforts. Flag days, parties, entertainments, fêtes, fairs, all were patronised. Funds were raised for Lord Robert Workshops, the District Nursing Association, Youth Club Equipment, Welfare of the Blind, Earl Haig's Poppy Fund, Red Cross, Relief of Larissa, the Lord Mayor of London's National Air Raid Distress Fund, Russian Relief, the Ex-Servicemen's Welfare Association, Merchant Navy Comforts' Fund, Warships' Week, Y.W.C.A. Fund for Women in H.M. Forces, St. Alban's Diocesan Fund, Parcels for Russian Soldiers, a named bed in Stalingrad Hospital, and the contributions of cash and clothing to Dr Barnardo's Homes, the evacuees next door, and other needy groups in Bedford.

Agricultural camps

Nor did war effort cease at the end of the Summer term for throughout the war parties of girls helped in the agricultural camps: in 1942 four weeks were spent at Bourne, Kesteven, by two sets of 22 girls and 3 mistresses who each worked for a fortnight. The following year from 40–45 girls at a time took part in lifting potatoes, while in 1944 the quarters were in the Carre's Grammar School, Sleaford, and the work flax pulling for three weeks, and potato lifting for the last. The fourth and last camp was at Hacconby near Bourne, Lincolnshire where potato lifting and thistle spudding were the chief jobs. Miss Pugh, as a Guider with some experience of camping, was a regular staff member and gives a vivid picture.

'Viewed in retrospect the conditions were appalling but we were prepared to put up with anything to be able to help our country. What I mean will be clearer if I describe our first "camp". I went with Miss De la Mare and Miss Angus and about 30 girls, and Mrs Wilkins (mother of Joan and Barbara) to cook for us. We had an old mission hall to sleep in: it had a tiny kitchen with a large gas stove and sink. The lavatories were outside and consisted of two cubicles with seats over large pails: nearby a deep hole had been dug with a heap of lime near. Each morning after the girls had gone to work, the staff would carry the full pails, empty them in the pit and cover the contents with soil and lime. The girls were provided with straw-filled mattress covers and slept on the floor in the hall. The staff had two tents on the bit of grass outside the hall, and had camp beds. We rose at 6.30 a.m. The girls piled their mattresses on the platform of the hall and put up trestle tables on which were placed tin bowls of water for washing. When these were cleared, the tables were laid for breakfast consisting of porridge, bread and butter and marmalade. Then, gathering up their packed lunch prepared the night before, the girls climbed into a bus to go to work: usually at least one member of staff went with them.

'During the day, after the sanitation had been dealt with, a good bit of time was spent preparing the hot evening meal. We had marvellous extra rations: each week we had a whole ham – unheard of in the world outside! – and splendid joints of meat and lashings of extra cheese and butter. As well as food preparation, there was also tidying up and shopping, and so on.

'The girls returned about 4.30–5.00 p.m., very hot and dusty, but were only able to have a "hot wash", before they had their meal. After that was cleared, at one end of the table slices of bread and sandwich contents were laid out and they prepared their lunch for next day – no plastic bags either! Then the tables were taken down and the mattresses put out. There was not much time or energy for recreation except on Saturday evening and Sunday.

'This was the most primitive place we were in. The next year we were in an old Maltings but I was not able to go so cannot speak of it. The year after, we were in the boys' Grammar School in Spalding where the girls slept on the floor in the hall and the Staff in the classroom. For two years after that we were in a nice little manor house just outside Bourne: this was the best billet we had. It was not big but there was just enough room for us all. The cooking was done on a large oil stove and we had the school cook to cook for us and the food was excellent.

'The work was mostly potato picking, though we did do a bit of fruit picking and weeding sugar beet. The potato lifting was back-aching work. A machine called a "spinner" turned up rows of potatoes and they had to be picked up by hand and put into baskets. On some farms a cart went along and took the baskets to the riddles, which sieved out the dust and small tubers, but sometimes we had to carry the heavy baskets to the riddle ourselves. A basic wage was paid but bonuses were added at so much per hundredweight over a minimum and some girls earned what were quite princely sums in those days.'

Old Girls in wartime

Old Girls, too, took their active share in the war effort; at school, where they shared in the fire-watching and throughout the country, as well as in the Forces. Particular mention was made in the 1946 'O.G. News' (the first issue since 1939) of Betty Wilkins, who as a Q.A.I.M.N.S. served in India, and Kathleen Hutton, also a Q.A.I.M.N.S., who was flown from Rangoon to Central Burma, where she and another Sister were stationed with a small mobile forward Field Hospital. Later she was moved again to be one of the first British women to fly to Bangkok, Siam, where she had charge of a large India ward with 80 beds. Frances Wright was also actively involved, though in a different way. She was 'called to the Bar' as a member of Gray's Inn in June 1942. As she intended practising abroad in her home in Sierra Leone, she had to go down to the Law Courts and sign the Roll of Barristers, otherwise she would not have the right to practise abroad. After this she worked as a Barrister in the Temple for about 10 months and then two months later started for home. On the voyage to Sierra Leone her ship was torpedoed. She had a narrow escape, was in an open boat for some time, and lost all her belongings. Before taking up her post as a Junior to her father and another Barrister, special permission had to be obtained from the Chief Justice to appear in the Supreme Court without her wig and gown as these had gone down with all her things.

Teaching in wartime

Back in Bedford, the staff were involved in the strains of fire-watching by day and night, term and holidays for two years, problems of supply for the Boarding House, which had to be closed down in July 1944, and the girls accommodated for the time being in private homes, the stress of ever increasing numbers, staff illnesses and problems of replacement. One marvels at the resilience and strength of Miss Tonkin and her devoted band of established teachers. That was not all. During these years, debate was in progress on the whole concept of education leading to the 1944 Butler Act, and in 1944 Miss Tonkin co-operated in an 'Extension of School Life' scheme which led to the admission of 19 girls aged 12–14 who would not otherwise have stayed at school beyond the then legal leaving age of 14. They must have posed problems in almost every subject and complicated the already complex timetable.

In all this activity, the basic work of the school proceeded without wavering. Its first purpose was to educate; to open to each new generation the doors of learning through which their predecessors had passed to a fulfilled and happy life. Even the examination effort was maintained. At the distribution of certificates in December 1939, there were six girls who had taken, with rather limited success, the Higher School Certificate examination, four more had been content with subsidiary subjects; 29 had obtained School Certificates of whom 9 matriculated. In November 1945, five girls had obtained a full Higher Certificate and one a Subsidiary Certificate; 52 had gained their school certificates, 26 of them with Matriculation Exemption. There were three V forms – Science, Language and Lower, and the school was organised as a three stream entry school with a Preparatory Department. In 1939 it had been a two stream school. Numbers in the classes also rose during these years, so that the teaching burden became heavier.

What the school owes to the devoted staff of those years it is hard to express. First to the seniors, Miss Baldwin, Miss Pugh, Mrs Matkin, Miss Carter, Miss Cranmer, Miss Grattan, Miss Window, Miss Lewis, and Miss Knight in the office. Each of them deeply committed to her vocation; able and progressive teachers, lively and outgoing personalities, offering to their pupils both an adventure into knowledge and a stable and secure moral background, an assurance in the darkest days that faith and hope would prevail. Then to that galaxy of younger women who came and went, or stayed to form the nucleus of an equally devoted post-war staff with the survivors from pre-war days. It was a happy, friendly staff room, never too busy to laugh together, always giving to the school far more than could be required of them. In the Diamond Jubilee Service in May 1942 a special prayer gave thanks 'for the devoted service of those who have taught in this place, for their words of life, for their understanding hearts and their abiding influence'. They were indeed greatly to be thanked.

The end of the War

The success of the D-Day landings of 1944 made ultimate victory certain, and by the autumn of that year the B.B.C. was making plans for the celebration of a cease-fire. On 5th October Leslie Woodgate wrote to Miss Tonkin, asking if 50 of the girls would help in the production of a new work by Vaughan Williams. Fifty boys from B.M.S. were already promised and he wrote, 'The music is not difficult and as the Anthem will be broadcast on Victory Day, I feel sure that you would like your girls to represent the children of England singing in this work.' It was a great honour for the school, and the girls acquitted themselves well under Sir Adrian Boult's baton. Some of the hymns and *Land of Hope and Glory* were featured in the *Children's Hour* programme on V.E. Day, 8th May and the Vaughan Williams *Victory Anthem* was heard at the broadcast service on the following Sunday. At least once in its history, the school's notable music making has spoken for the nation.

V.E. Day, and a school holiday; what inexpressible relief it was for all the adults of the community; what light hearted, whole-hearted rejoicing for all. Happily Miss Tonkin planned a service of thanksgiving for their return.

'Not unto us, O Lord, not unto us
But unto thy Name give glory
For thy mercy and thy truth's sake.'

Hundreds of schools did the same; the whole people enjoyed the temporary euphoria of peace.

The effort remained; six days later the 'Special Place' examination took place. Next the O.G.A. – put into cold storage when war started – was to be revived. The Gymnastics Competitions took place and the public examinations were held. It was good to celebrate their end by taking the Seniors to London, now free of black-out, to see *Hamlet*; gracious of the senior girls to hold a party for the staff who had seen them through the years of endeavour.

There was a sense of new beginnings in education and the Sixth form spent some time on a project planning and working out a new kind of school for Bedford to fit in with the requirements of the Butler Act. This new 'Modern' school, destined in their words 'to serve the interests both of the child and of the nation' should have a twofold aim. 'On the one hand the children must be prepared, to some extent, for their future work and given a broad outlook upon it, and on the other hand they must be taught how to make the best of life.'

Miss Tonkin retires

In 1945 Miss Tonkin was 61 years of age. For twenty years she had directed, cared for and guided the school. Her health was beginning to suffer from the continuous strain. After years in which she had always been present, she had been absent for part of the Spring term 1944 and a year later, Miss Pugh was appointed Acting Headmistress to cover the interregnum following on Miss Tonkin's resignation at Christmas. At her wish, news of her impending departure had been muted until the end of the Christmas term, when every organisation associated with the school in turn tried to express its feelings of desolation at her going. She had been a greatly loved Headmistress and the memory of her style and her principles remained with the school for many years and still lives in the minds of ex-staff and Old Girls today. Tributes in the Magazine were deeply felt. A former member of staff wrote, 'With her, philosophy, religion, education and work of all kinds were woven indivisibly into a way of life in which all shared in creating a fundamental harmony. The atmosphere of sympathetic understanding, tolerance and helpful consideration gave that feeling of security which encourages the best development of each individual. No one sought her sympathy or advice in vain; her time, her wise counsel and her practical help were always freely given to those in any trouble or difficulty, while her rich sense of humour lightened many an anxious moment, especially during the years of war.'

Her relations with the Governors had always been harmonious and in a tribute, one of them wrote, 'The most striking feature about Miss Tonkin was the contrast between her remarkably traditional appearance and her completely personal and unconventional approach to every situation. She showed always and in all circumstances an absolute faith in the power of right personal relations to deal adequately with all situations which could arise, and her influence with the Governors, the staff, and the girls of the school was undoubtedly conditioned by this faith . . . It is insufficiently realised in these days to how great an extent education, in the true sense of the word, is a matter of personality, and the example and influence of Miss Tonkin, in all the circles in which she moved, were of incalculably great educational value, precisely because of her great gift for working on and through personality.'

The staff, past and present, at her going presented her with a magnificent hand bound volume, listing the contributors to a cheque and handbag, and including three exquisite water-colours of the new school. The delicacy and imaginativeness of the illumination and the charm of the sketches are themselves a tribute to the sensitivity of the recipient and the percipience of the givers and the artist who devoted so much time to the task. Its final message, appropriately for a linguist was in Latin – 'Ob omnia quae pro nobis fecisti, quodque nobis cara es, gratias tibi agimus.'

In Cardington Road – The Dame Alice Harpur School

Post-War problems

The immediate post-war period was not likely to prove easy for a new Headmistress. In the country at large there was a deep rooted feeling that children had missed so much during the years of war that they must be indulged and deferred to. Years of special treatment under rationing had made them the most important section of the community. It was the beginning of the cult of youth. At the same time the implementation of the Butler Act, which increased the domination of the 11+ over primary education, was at odds with the liberalisation of work in the Infants' Schools. During the war, great difficulties had been caused by the coming and going of children into and from safe areas and the consequent problems of accommodating many who had started on different syllabuses or methods of work. It was an age of full employment; able women had seen many new opportunities and spheres of work opened to them, and it was not easy to find an adequate replacement for Miss Tonkin.

The coming of Miss Forster

Nevertheless, from forty-nine applicants for the post, of whom eight were short-listed, the choice fell upon Miss Irene L. Forster, who at forty-three was an experienced headmistress.

After attending schools in Birmingham and Glasgow, she had gone from Cheltenham Ladies' College to Bedford College, London, and gained her B.Sc. in Pure and Applied Mathematics and Physics in 1924, and then in 1926 specialised in Physics, gaining a B.Sc. in Physics in 1927. She had held posts as an assistant mistress in Notting Hill High School, King's High School, Warwick, the Princess Mary High School, Halifax and a senior science post at Haberdashers' Aske's School before becoming Headmistress of Wellington High School for Girls in

1939. Here she had faced problems of re-organisation both of space and syllabus and an increase in numbers from 230 to 390. She had founded a Parent-Teacher Association and an Old Girls' Association, while in the town she had been connected with the Youth Club and was a member of the Juvenile Committee of the Ministry of Labour. Her mother's profession was music, and through her Miss Forster had many personal connections in the music world, which she hoped to use for the benefit of the school by having concerts, lectures and dramatic performances.

Her letter to the Old Girls in the 1946 'News' gives us an idea of her first impressions. 'I have enjoyed my first term in Bedford very much indeed, chiefly owing to the friendliness of all connected with the school, – staff, girls, parents, Old Girls and others. I had heard before I arrived of the delightful atmosphere prevailing at the school, and the reports I had had were not exaggerated. My predecessors have indeed built up a school of which they must be justly proud and one to which it is a joy to come. . . . You would probably like to know something of what the school is doing at present and what its hopes are for the future. The numbers grow apace. We expect some 600 girls this coming term (Sept. '46), of whom 50 to 60 will be in Form VI. This form, to the great benefit of the whole school, has been growing fast recently, and more and more girls are staying to take the Higher Certificate while others spend one or two years studying more general subjects. We have girls hoping to take up careers which include Agriculture, Art, Dispensing, Domestic Science, Laboratory work, Law, Medicine, Music, Nursing, Pharmacy, Physical Training, Secretarial work, Social work and teaching of various kinds. Most of these will proceed to a university or college of some kind to prepare for their chosen career. With an entry of over one hundred new girls each year, it seems as if the sixth form should be even larger soon.

Her problems and plans

'But where are these 600 to be housed in a building designed for 350? I suppose we shall squeeze in somehow next term, but every available corner will be occupied and there are forms in the laboratories and other rooms which are quite unsuitable for classrooms. We have a permit for a "hut" which will make two classrooms, but when it will be available we have no idea. Plans are on foot for starting the teaching of Cookery again as soon as possible, but this, too, needs a new hut and equipment. We hope also to have a school boarding home again in the near future.

'We are going to organise the library so that all girls, from their entry into the main school at the age of about eleven, can have easy access to it, and we are arranging a junior section of it containing works of fiction and other books suitable for the younger girls.

'We are able to increase the number of music lessons for most forms and to have most forms taught separately because we have an additional full-time member of staff joining us in September, Mr Freyhan, who will teach Music and German. Having both Miss Huntington and Mr Freyhan will make it possible, in course of time, to have school choirs and perhaps an orchestra and other musical activities we hope.

'Before long you may hear that the school has a new name. We may be known as The Dame Alice Harpur School, if the Minister of Education gives her approval to our choice. The term "Modern" having acquired a special meaning since the recent Education Act was enforced, we feel that the old name is misleading to people from other parts of the country who do not necessarily know that we are a 'grammar' school of long standing. . . .' So Miss Forster outlined some of the problems and plans which were to occupy her in her career as Headmistress from 1946 to 1955.

Effects of the 1944 Education Act

For the Governors of the Harpur Trust, however, the 1944 Act brought a different problem. Their principal object was to provide education for boys and girls. To this end they had co-operated with the County Council in providing free places at the four schools for suitable scholars from the county as well as the town, and when in 1919 the schools became Direct Grant schools, the proportion of free places was fixed at 25 per cent of the year's intake for the Boys' and Girls' Modern Schools, but only 10 per cent for Bedford School and the High School. (Both the County Council and the Borough were represented on the Trust from 1919.) Since for the greater part of the county the

Harpur Trust schools were the only grammar schools, the County Council were anxious that all four schools should offer the higher percentage of free places as expressed in the 1944 Act – i.e. up to 50%: only thus they felt would there be the required number of free grammar school places for all the qualified pupils in their catchment area.

The Harpur Trust was ready to help the L.E.A. to extend the range of secondary education but to accept 50% free places in each year's intake would obviously, particularly at Bedford School and the High School, affect the composition of the schools. They had already achieved a more than nation-wide reputation for their high standards of education, and it was felt that the wide variety of locality and background of the pupils was of considerable educational value to them.

Financially, too, all concerned were anxious for agreement. The County Council had greatly benefited from the 1919 arrangements. In 1923 it was noted that the average County Council expenditure in England per head of day scholars receiving secondary education was £17: while in Durham it was as high as £26, in Bedfordshire it was as low as £6. The Harpur Trust, too, had benefited from the Direct Grant system. In 1942 the four schools maintained approximately 2,400 pupils at an average cost (taken over the years 1940, '41, '42,) of £86,000. During those years the average income from the Government Direct Grant was £20,674, and from the County Council £9,240, leaving a balance to meet from fees and the endowment of £56,000 (approx). War damage to the Holborn property had led to a fall in the endowment; from about £22,000 (pre-war figures) to £3,890 in 1943.

The ultimate solution to the problem led to Bedford School and the High School becoming independent, the 10 per cent free places in both remaining and being taken up by the L.E.A., while the Modern Schools remained Direct Grant schools, the 50 per cent statutory free places increased to cope with the demands of the L.E.A. (up to 80 per cent in the case of BGMS/DAHS) until the opening of Stratton School, Biggleswade somewhat relieved the pressure.

The effect of the 1944 Education Act on the school itself was not to create new problems so much as to intensify those already existing. As soon as 'county' girls had begun to attend school, the problems of daily travel with the difficulties caused by fog or snow, or later by strikes, had had to be taken into consideration. When afternoon lessons became usual, the provisions of a hot midday meal, and a recreation room had been suggested, and Dame Alice House (East Lodge) finally bought for this purpose.

It was more difficult for girls who had to travel to stay later in the afternoon for extra-curricular activities such as Games, and Guide meetings. With the increase of the statutory 25 per cent Free Place entry to 50 per cent, (the actual percentage was much greater), far more girls came within this category, and all these intensified problems had to be faced and overcome.

For the girls who travelled, standing on overcrowded buses – the 'double-deckers' with their open platforms and very little heating – was part of the daily routine. 'Learning' homework could still be done – there were many volunteer 'hearers'. Train travel offered the advantage of being able to do written homework as well, but whether by bus or train – 'Bletchley Line' or 'Midland Road' – the stories told were manifold, and the problems little considered.

More space required

With all this it was obvious that expansion was still necessary, and in the post-war economic situation this was difficult. When the new school in Cardington Road was planned it was felt that to provide for 330 places was sufficient, although this was increased to 360 (1935). By 1941, with the number at 504, Miss Tonkin reported: 'Although the building was planned for 360, it is so spacious that it is not badly overcrowded', but by September 1946 Miss Forster was asking 'Where shall we put 600? . . .'

The Huts

The 'huts' came first, at the edge of the playing field, reached by a roofed but open-sided corridor with brick pillars and steep steps either side from a door near the gymnasium. In these the Sixth form were housed at first, but they later became the abode of middle school forms. Slightly isolated from the main school, there was a feeling of 'one-ness' with those more energetically employed on the playing field, held more particularly by those in the row nearest those windows. The memories of former inhabitants range from the chill of winter days alleviated by the stove (also used for roasting chestnuts) in one corner, the electrically heated pipes which were later guarded by grilles after many a leg had suffered from too close contact, the murals by which the walls in one hut were decorated by an enterprising IVth, and the idea later copied in the other, to the variety of uses to which the steps of the connecting corridor could be put, particularly in the dinner hour.

The 'huts' freed one room in the school, and allowed the waiting room to be used by the matron as a sickroom and store, but as Miss Forster wrote in her 1946–47 Report: 'The forms are nearly all too large. There are two of 40 girls, two of 39 girls, two of 38, and two of 37, and the rest are not much smaller. Two laboratories and the Geography Room are still used as form rooms. (Memories of lack of storage space for textbooks and satchels piled on the floor.) Moreover, we generally have four science lessons at the same time, and a fourth science room is badly needed. The use of the Recreation Room in Dame Alice House for music will probably not be so possible when the new dining arrangements are made.'

Dining problems

One of the main reasons for acquiring Dame Alice House (formerly East Lodge) had been its provision of dining and recreation rooms for the use of country girls. Special arrangements had been made throughout the war, but in the Autumn term, 1944, Miss Tonkin reported: 'We are now starting to cook as well as serve hot dinners on the premises. We have had to make considerable structural alterations in the kitchen to facilitate cooking for the estimated 200–250 meals daily . . . We have had to engage a special kitchen staff, cook, assistant cook, vegetable hands, but I hope that with the continued subsidy from the Ministry of Education we shall be able to provide a really appetising and nourishing meal at the price of 6d per dinner.' By September in the following year numbers had risen to 350 and there were, in addition, nearly 100 who brought their own lunch. Thus about 450 of the 582 pupils were staying at school for lunch. Though there was a drop in the numbers of girls bringing their own lunch, the numbers of those having the school dinner did not fall below 350 and to meet the demand 40 dinners were sent into school, first by the British Restaurant and then by the L.E.A., until the opening of the Boarding House in 1950 meant that 40 girls could receive dinner there. Not until the Summer term of 1954 was the Abbey ready to be used for dining for all those requiring hot dinner – by this time 460.

The dining room in Dame Alice House with its French windows opening on to the garden looks very pleasant in a photograph taken in the early days, with its tables each seating 6–8 girls. Far different was its appearance with 360 girls to feed. The individual tables were replaced by long tables, with girls sitting on forms or chairs of all patterns, as many as possible squeezed along each side. 'We queued up in the tunnel at the foot of the

stairs, and after the dining room was initially filled were allowed in, in proportion to those coming out. Those who came for second sitting had to line up at the second bell at 1.20 p.m. As a girl, to me, the amount of noise was something quite remarkable; what it was like in the staff dining room on the left at the top of the stairs, can be imagined. Once up the stairs we turned right, collected our first course from the hatch, our cutlery from the boxes, and entered the dining room by the door facing the staircase, and looked for a gap along the tables: this often had to be reached by climbing on to the row of chairs or forms, and by walking behind those already seated until the gap was reached, when we placed our plates on the table and scrambled into position. When the first course was eaten, we filed past the mistress on duty at the exit, who inspected the plates (to see that no good food was wasted), and our dinner tickets. (I can remember Miss Wells with Thisbe, her pet duck, at her side, and dreading being detained lest Thisbe should take a peck at my ankles!) If both were satisfactory, we proceeded to collect the second course from the hatch and repeat the process (except for dinner ticket inspection.)'

Linked with this system was the washing up duty in which six girls a day were on duty wiping up either cutlery or plates so that there were enough for the 'second-comers' to use for their meal. The 40 girls who had their dinner sent in dealt with their own washing up: those who were selected to go to the Boarding House were also freed from the general chore. They had to walk in crocodile to Margaret House in Bushmead Avenue where they had their meal more formally with grace at the beginning, and their meal served to them at small tables. On the way back to school, discipline was relaxed, the 'crocodile' disappeared, and girls made their way in a more leisurely manner, each table leaving as its members finished. Wherever the meal was taken, the chief requirement for all girls seemed to be speed. Miss Forster, reporting to the Governors in September 1950, said: 'There is very great need for a new large dining room where girls can have their meals in proper sittings, instead of the present makeshift system which is bad training socially.'

The Abbey, '48' and '46'

In *Uisage* of the following September, Miss Forster was able to give the news of the purchase of the Abbey hotel, and the hope that it would be able to be used from January onwards. The foreword in the 1952 number of the *Uisage* stated: 'At the end of the Spring term we took possession of the Abbey, and a band of cleaners made the hall and two small rooms not only habitable, but attractive. The first occupants were music staff and their pupils, and very soon the more imaginative of the Preparatory Department had invented a ghost, whose attributes and activities have increased daily since then. In the Summer term we increased the numbers in the "Prep" to seventy-five and made three forms instead of two. Prep. I, in the charge of Miss Fernie, was installed in the "Tuscany Lounge" of the hotel. Miss Todman and Prep. II were brought across from Dame Alice House to what will eventually be part of the dining room . . . Mrs Horn and Prep. III remained in the old Lower I room but are likely to move soon, for now we have the news that we shall also probably have the use of number 48, the house next door to Dame Alice House, and may begin to use it in September. The addition of number 48 will mean . . . the sixth form will probably have the present dining room and other rooms, so that the present huts can be used for other forms and our congestion much relieved.'

Not until 1953 was it possible to transfer the dining room and kitchen to the Abbey, but by the time the 1954 *Uisage* was published, members of the sixth form could write: 'Already we are beginning to take for granted the increased space and facilities which "Kilpin House" and "The Abbey" have given to the school . . . The most obvious benefit is probably the new dining room, with its heraldic windows, which enables us to eat our mid-day dinner in a reasonably civilised and leisurely manner: a great luxury to the many of us who grew up in a serve-yourself queue.'

The last addition to the school, number 46, soon known as Wing House, came when Miss Forster had announced her intention of retiring at Easter 1955. Its acquisition meant that the new school now owned all the houses between the Abbey and the main school, and provided an immediate answer to the problems of post-war expansion in numbers.

Doubtless for all the houses, the activities of the 1950s were very different from those of previous years. While for ordinary class teaching many of the rooms were difficult, for smaller divisions of older girls, and more especially for Modern Language work, the extra rooms were much appreciated. The Preparatory Department was able to expand; for a short time in the Abbey, then to Kilpin, where, in addition to the extra rooms, the orchard offered a delightful playground of which the 'Preps.' made imaginative use. The VI form enjoyed the increased freedom that separation from the rest of the school gave: the greater informality of lessons seemed aided by the atmosphere of the older houses, reflecting an age of greater leisure and quieter living than the mid-twentieth century. Music, too, needed room to expand, and first in the Abbey and then in Kilpin – the 'Music House' – rooms were found for teaching and practising instruments, as well as class and group singing. So the houses came to play their part in the general development of the school.

Academic developments

The situation educationally was far different when Miss Forster was appointed from that which had prevailed when Miss Dolby, at her first parents' meeting, had had to defend the need for sound education for girls. Now a sound education was being publicly demanded, and the task of a headmistress was to keep abreast of opinion, and to take full advantage of all that was being offered to make that education fitting for the wider opportunities that were now open to girls. 'Development' and 'expansion' rather than complete change were to be the keynote of the ensuing years, though the greater stress on good academic standards meant that some subjects had to be dropped.

The VI form Commercial Course, which Miss Knight had come to teach almost thirty years before in 1917, disappeared. From 1918 the O.G.A. leaflets list the examination successes in these subjects with a special note in January 1920: 'In both 1918 and 1919, Pupils from the Commercial Class have taken the Examinations of the Royal Society of Arts and the Midland Union of Educational Institutions in Shorthand, Book-keeping and Commercial Correspondence, with very satisfactory results.' By 1925, girls were taking the examination of the

London Chamber of Commerce; in that year two girls gained their full Junior Certificate, while several others gained a certificate in five or more subjects. Though the number of girls taking the course was always small, successes continued, eighteen girls gaining certificates, some with distinctions in several subjects, by 1934. One notable success was Miriam Dix who, in the Jubilee Year, gained a Full Certificate with distinctions in Arithmetic, Geography, Mathematics, English, Shorthand, French and Spanish. In 1938, the Royal Society of Arts examinations were again taken, and by 1944 sixteen more girls had gained the School Commercial Certificate.

After the 1944 Education Act it was clear that, since the school was the only Direct Grant Grammar School for girls in the area, its main responsibility was to achieve good academic standards and develop Sixth form work commensurate with Direct Grant status. (Qualifications for careers, such as the Commercial course had offered, would have therefore to be obtained out of school: they could not be fitted into the syllabus.) This, with its attendant problems, was Miss Forster's task.

The acquisition of the 'houses' gradually eased the pressure on the main school building, but during the early years, small divisions, especially of VI form, could find themselves having lessons in very unlikely places: the library store, the staff dining room in Dame Alice House, or even the storeroom under the back stairs, though this was very cramped and cold. Nevertheless work went on apace.

Beginning of Sixth form expansion

Three-form entry had begun in 1943: by 1948 there were three parallel forms at each stage of the main school below the VI form, except in the second year, where owing to the large numbers, there had to be four. Numbers in the VI form rose from 30 in 1943 to 52 in 1948, while in Miss Forster's last year the combined VI form numbers reached 95. Of those 54 in the first year VI, 20 or so were only intending to stay for a one year course, some to gain more examination qualifications and some until they had reached the qualifying age to enable them to pursue their chosen career elsewhere. In 1949 the average leaving age was 16 years 7 months: an encouraging fact in that it indicated that most girls were staying to complete the fifth year and taking the Cambridge School Certificate examination. There had been 200 entries in the years 1946–48 and 157 awards. It did mean, however, that most parents were still not regarding a Sixth form course as an integral part of a girl's school career. The legal school leaving age was still fixed at fifteen, and to stay even for five years meant for many girls one extra year, and some financial sacrifice, probably more so among families in rural areas, i.e. those of some 50% of Dame Alice pupils. To these the rewards of an extra two years in the VI form were as yet not obvious enough, unless a girl's chosen career needed the qualifications offered and warranted the sacrifice. Thus from 1946–48 the relatively small total of 34 girls sat for the Higher School Certificate, of whom 26 were successful. Two of these, however, in 1948 gained State Scholarships and were among the 15 who entered universities in this three-year period. Nevertheless the numbers in the VI form by the time Miss Forster left show that things were beginning to change, albeit slowly.

At the lower end of the school expansion also took place. The Preparatory or Junior Department which had been much handicapped by the shortage of accommodation was able, on the acquisition of the Abbey, to increase its numbers from fifty to eighty, in three forms, (Preps. I and II and III instead of Transition and Lower I). It was to become even larger in September 1955 when a fourth form was added, I Remove, and Kilpin House became their home.

The actual curriculum changed little. Latin was re-introduced in 1946 as an alternative to German as the second language in the second year: the lack of Latin had proved a hindrance to several VI form girls in gaining university entrance. The erection of the long-awaited Domestic Science 'hut' in 1949 meant that that subject could be again practised by groups of forms IV, V, and VI, while in the same year Greek was introduced for small numbers of the V and VI forms. The great change was referred to by Miss Forster in her foreword of *Uisage* 1950.

The new G.C.E.

'We have seen the passing of the School and Higher School Certificate examinations. Twelve of our sixteen candidates for the latter were successful, and fifty-four out of seventy-five in the former. In the new General Certificate of Education which replaces them, we are determined to try to achieve a record of which we can be proud. The new scheme offers much scope for individual choice of subject in the fifth and sixth forms, giving opportunity to each to develop her work as is best for her. We hope that more and more will take advantage of the more advanced work which they can do if they stay in Form VI . . . We hope that all girls, at whatever stage of their school careers, will set their minds on achieving a high standard of work, remembering Mr Guy Pocock's words (Speech Day 1950) that they are here, not to be educated, but to educate themselves. . . .'

The increase in the number of girls in 1951–55 taking both Ordinary and Advanced Level examinations shows that many more were taking advantage of the opportunities to gain a 'good' General Certificate. Many were also inspired by the staff of these years with a love of a subject which has deepened into a real appreciation later on in their lives, and provided many happy memories of schooldays.

Memories of staff and lessons

A few are given:

'In Transition Miss Huntington took us for Music and Singing in a long room with a creaking floor. She used to stand us on a table to sing solos to her, and we made music stands from clay and split canes. There was a percussion performance of the *Egyptian Ballet*, and a costume performance of *Peter and the Wolf* . . . with the tree represented by a large stepladder in the middle of the stage.'

'. . . Miss Ware practising phonetics with us in our early French lessons, our rather "home-made" sound compared with her accuracy. I am still trying to achieve this accuracy!'

'Mrs Long introduced us to Shakespeare, starting with *A Midsummer Night's Dream*. She "made" us believe in the characters . . .' 'Mrs Walker, whose English lessons I remember so vividly, especially Shakespeare. I think we began with *The Merchant of Venice* but I can still quote many of the passages we learnt from *Julius Caesar*, *Macbeth*, and *Richard III*.'

'I wonder if Miss Wells is still in Bedford? I so enjoyed the two years in the studio in her charge. I wouldn't have missed the Art History course for anything. Such a pity one rarely realises *at the time* the significance of certain stages in one's life. I was so interested in the Italian Renaissance – but we studied the French Impressionists too. They left me "cold", but Miss Wells was enthusiastic. Some years later when living in Switzerland I went to an exhibition of Impressionist paintings. The colours blazed from the canvases. What I had been taught in the classroom suddenly fell into place.'

Many have mentioned Miss Broadway's History lessons, her ability to set the scene and bring the characters to life, and Miss Burnell and her activities in the Gymnasium and on the playing field, her encouragement of good posture, and her teaching and demonstration of the art of relaxation. They have spoken of the kindly patience of the Mathematics teachers, Miss Pengilly, Mrs Gray and Mrs Childs, who were later joined by Miss Southwell whose enthusiasm communicated itself to many. The Science staff, Miss Pugh, Miss Jackson, Miss Flood, and Miss Forster herself had the task of introducing what was to many an unknown and somewhat awesome subject, Science, taught in a laboratory with its complex equipment and peculiar smells.

Some of these long-serving staff had come during the war years, or just after: Miss Pengilly, who, besides teaching Mathematics, served as the first Careers mistress, and also as Second mistress: Miss Rooth, who took on librarian's duties as well as English, and was responsible for the first rearrangement and re-cataloguing of the books: Miss Burnell, Mrs Horn of Lower I (later I Remove), and Miss Wells, who as an 'Old Girl', proved a worthy successor to Mrs Matkin in opening the world of Art to all her pupils, helping the talented to realise their full potential but also inspiring and assisting the less-gifted to realise the satisfaction of achievement at their own level. Many, however, owed their appointments to Miss Forster herself, of whom it was reported that she had a fine judgment in choosing staff. Miss Todman in the Prep. Department came in 1946, with Miss Sas, beloved as a form-mistress as well as a teacher of French for twenty-six years, while 1947 saw the arrival of Miss Helliwell (16 years), Miss Broadway (28 years), Miss Jackson (25 years), Miss Stonebridge (14 years). Miss Arnot (16 years) came in

1948, Miss Höcker (20 years), Miss Key (25 years), Mrs Childs (24 years full-time, still teaching part-time 1982) and Miss Carr (7 years) in 1949, while Mrs Walker, earlier part-time teacher in the English Department, taught full-time from 1949–63. In 1953, Miss Southwell was appointed to be Head of Mathematics, and served until 1978. All these, together with many colleagues who served in junior posts for shorter periods, made the routine of lessons an adventure in learning. They also gave their time and enthusiasm to school plays such as *Lady Precious Stream* in 1947, House and form activities, clubs and societies including a school branch of C.E.W.C. and a Debating Society, as well as being involved in an expanding musical and sporting programme, and expeditions of all kinds.

Expanding activities

Selections from *Uisage* give an idea of this growing activity. 'At the beginning of the Easter term the Science Society was formed for the benefit of senior girls who stayed to dinner. Meetings have been held regularly every Wednesday since then. The members of the society have made many interesting specimens, including soap, fireworks, nail varnish, chemical gardens and dyes. During the Summer term we have assembled some useful and amusing pieces of apparatus, such as an electrical writing set, an iron lung and an apparatus for making smoke screens. Miss Pugh gave a short talk on blood groups and afterwards, much to our delight, we were able to test our own blood. Miss Pugh and Miss Dodd took the members on a very interesting visit to the Brewery in July . . . The Society has proved immensely popular and our thanks are due to Miss Kett, Miss Pugh and Miss Dodd for their untiring help and enthusiasm.' – September 1948 issue.

'The French class went to London with Miss Cranmer and Miss Baldwin. We were all away from school at the time, due to the floods, but Miss Cranmer managed to get in touch with all of us. In the morning we went to see the exhibition of Spanish pictures at the National Gallery and in the afternoon Rostand's *Cyrano de Bergerac*, one of our set books, performed by Ralph Richardson and the Old Vic Company at the New Theatre.'

'The first proposal for a gardening club was put to the School

Council last Christmas term and was carried. Miss Hunt kindly agreed to take charge, and the club was open to all forms. The girls were divided into groups and the work allotted included: cleaning and general tidying of King's Ditch (a delight to the juniors), caring for Dame Alice House garden, the side front garden, and the rose garden, and helping in the vegetable garden. Our work was interrupted by the floods, which came just when the garden had taken on some semblance of tidiness. Then we lost Miss Hunt, and the club enthusiasm decreased. On returning to school after the floods, we found the garden in a chaotic state. Weeds were abundant and pieces of stick, mud and silt covered everything. Members of the club were called together, and slowly the garden has improved . . . If it is possible we should like to make a lawn with shady trees on what is now the raised ground between the hockey pitch and the river . . . The gardening club provided a really good way of keeping warm during dinner hours in the winter and we need more members.'

The 1947 floods

1947 was to become known as the 'year of the flood'. There had been floods before, and have been since, but these affected not only the school but the surrounding areas of the town: Cardington Road was under water, and photographs in the school archives show milk being delivered by punt to the Abbey hotel, the residents leaning from the first floor windows to receive it. Miss Forster notes in her 'Log-book':

'March 14th – *The Great Flood* – school dismissed at 2 p.m. – water coming in under Compass Door. School cleared of things on ground floor.

'March 15th – Unable to get along Cardington Road in morning – came in high lorry in afternoon. 18 inches of water on ground floor.

'March 19th – V and VI forms at High School in afternoon.

'March 27th – Term ended because of floods – (instead of April 1st).'

Though the water subsided rapidly, the mud and other debris provided staff and girls with hours of scrubbing and mopping. The resultant damage was, however, less than had been feared, though for many years the mark showing the level of the flood water could be seen on the panelling in the hall and in the library. The description of the grounds given in the Hockey report, 'The season ended with the fields under water, one set of goalposts washed away, and the swans alone enjoying the desolate expanse,' has been echoed at intervals during succeeding winters, but the internal flooding has never been so severe since. The threat has remained, and sandbags have been used occasionally since as the illustration shows.

1948 activities

Gardening Club continued its activities in 1948, bringing under cultivation the bank near the river, which, as reported in *Uisage* was 'until recently a wilderness of weeds and stinging nettles.'

The Spring term of that year saw VI General's expedition to visit the Ideal Home Exhibition at Olympia, accompanied by Miss Pengilly. 'After standing in the train all the way, we arrived at St. Pancras and made our way to the exhibition. There we divided up and went off to explore. We were all extremely interested in the fashions, and some of us saw a mannequin parade of the "New Look". On the same floor as the fashions were cosmetics and hair styles, and also there was a special part roped off where were portrayed scenes from all the new films, set out with exquisitely made models. There was one scene which was particularly striking, and that was from the film, *Green for Danger*. . . . Great excitement was caused when some of our party said they had seen Joe Louis and his wife during their wanderings. . . . There was one stall, run by *The Girls' Own Paper* made to look like the teenager's ideal bedroom. There was a divan bed and a conveniently placed bookshelf and a radio which roused our envy. . .'

In July 1948, the V form had an expedition to London, dividing into groups on arrival: one made its way to the Science Museum in South Kensington where among other exhibits they saw the *Darkness into Daylight* exhibition: 'This was especially intriguing as we saw some of the marvellous lighting that will become available to the public in a few years.' Another group of nine, 'made our way by bus to Battersea Park. We spent a pleasant hour, armed with catalogue and camera, studying statuary in a most attractive setting. It was felt that, while Moore's figures gained from standing on a slight rise, and the Lake formed a delightful background for 'Spring', some pieces, such as 'The Visitation' lost something in a rural setting. Inside the enclosure, a group of students were giving a practical exhibition, and we saw examples of woodcarving, clay-modelling for casting, and work in stone.'

'Forty V formers visited University College Hospital accompanied by Mrs Long, Miss Baldwin and a friend . . . As the Matron was away we were welcomed by two Sisters and two

'Old Girls' who afterwards acted as our guides.' In groups of ten they visited the Ear, Nose and Throat, Maternity and Child Welfare, and Outpatients' Departments, – they found the latter very interesting. 'This hospital does not allow patients to wait for hours to see the doctors, but everyone has an appointment. It was about eleven forty-five when we reached this department and the sister told us that already two hundred patients had been interviewed. The out-patients' room was long and seats were arranged for those keeping appointments. A small canteen worked very efficiently in one corner, and in another was an office in which patients could discuss their problems of diet with dieticians. The almoners had their office here also.' They visited the Preliminary Training School, saw several wards, and actually viewed part of an operation through glass panels. Little wonder the visit was described as 'exciting, interesting, and instructive'. Perhaps, too, it is not surprising that when H.M. Inspectors visited the school in March 1949, they found that nursing was increasing in popularity as a career: in 1948 it drew 13 per cent of all leavers.

Development of field work

Visits to London proliferated: many, such as those to Wimbledon for the Wightman Cup matches, Wembley for the International Hockey, to Exhibitions at the Royal Academy, were to become annual events. Other visits which were to become annual were those made to the Field Study Centres by the VI form Biologists and Geographers. Flatford Mill was the first, visited in 1948 and 1949 to study the ecology of the Stow valley, while 1951 saw the Geographers in Derbyshire studying Geology, concluding their trip with a visit to a Sheffield steelworks.

'Every member of the party promptly named the spectacle that met her eyes "Dante's Inferno". It was so hot that we had to stand back, for fear of being melted like the steel, especially when they tapped a furnace, and the flying sparks rained all over us. Blue coloured glasses were handed to us so that we could look into the heat of the furnace with comfort, but there was nothing to prevent our bones from being shaken when the hydraulic hammer was working. Machine shops, tool shops, die-casting shops, followed in rapid confusing succession, mile after mile of noisy, clanking machinery; but our high pitched school voices stood us in good stead when we were forced to converse against the din.'

The growing emphasis on field work, one of the newer trends in post-war education, is reflected in these reports. A growing number of Field Centres, such as Flatford, catered particularly for this, providing laboratories, workrooms and a library, and often evening lectures from resident experts on the area. Field work could also be done using Youth Hostels as centres: in this way a variety of areas perhaps some distance apart could be studied, but obviously Youth Hostels did not provide the studying facilities of the Field Centres. It would certainly be difficult to say which offered the most unforgettable experiences.

Another 'annual' of these years was the VI form visit to the Sewage Farm: 'Imagine an icy cold day, with a strong wind, a two mile bicycle ride, a steep hill, a party of Sixth form girls with Miss Pugh and Miss Jackson, and you will have a mental picture of our visit to the Sewage Farm. We set out soon after lunch, toiled along the road and up the hill, until we were confronted by the gate of the Sewage Works. After depositing our bicycles we were shown round by Mr Belt, who gave a clear, interesting talk. After we had walked all round the farm, we retired to his office "out of the wind and the rain's way", and asked him question. His answers were very enlightening and gave us a picture of the problems concerning the pollution of rivers by uncooperative factories and other troubles with which a Sewage Farm has to deal.' – (1949 *Uisage*)

Re-establishment of links with Europe

Travel abroad features again after the war with 'VI Upper travels in France' in April 1947. 'After a smooth crossing the lights of Dieppe harbour twinkling across the bay gave us our first glimpse of France.... We were impressed most by the kindliness of the people, the oddity of the food, the openness of the 'Marché Noir' and a peculiar and characteristic smell which seems to associate itself with French towns and houses. . . . A month was not long enough to accustom us to the traffic which dashes madly along the wrong side of the road, hooting vigorously at every possible opportunity. Although we went to various districts, we all found difficulty in getting used to the late hours of entertainments, the odd and widely spaced meal times, and the wine with every dish. We thought that French meal-time conversations were generally more inspiring than their English counterpart.' The only mention made of the war was of 'Jean bathing in the mine-infested waters of war-scarred Le Havre.' This contrasts with the visit paid to Germany by Barbara Lawrence and Phyllis Uff (then VI_2) in July 1949. They spent 'seven weeks in a village near Kassel, a town in the American Zone of Germany. Our position was perhaps more unusual than we realised. The ban on tourist travel had been lifted only a few weeks before. For nearly a decade the ordinary people of Germany had known no friendly personal contacts with the ordinary people of England and America. German youth knew us only as conquerors, military squads that clattered down the streets and Commanders who occupied the best buildings – beflagged with the Stars and Stripes. The city centres were decaying heaps of uncleared ruins, skeleton houses, slowly crumbling, and the factories on which Germany's livelihood depended were steadily being dismantled. Yet in spite of this, although we were, as far as we know, the first tourists to visit Kassel for ten years, we found no shadow of hostility among the varied people with whom we came in contact. There was real kindness and interest everywhere we went.'

The 1950s saw the establishment of many connections abroad as well as the extension of travel to larger school parties. The growing interest was reflected in talks given to the P.T.A. in December 1952 by Miss Baldwin and Miss Höcker on 'Continental Education'. In the autumn of 1952 Dr Sandrock, a German Headmistress, had stayed with Miss Forster, spending time at 'Dame Alice' as well as visiting other schools in Bedford: in November 1952 Miss Forster had paid a return visit to Dr Sandrock's school, and she gave an account of this at the same P.T.A. meeting. Miss Höcker, after her appointment in 1950, fostered the connection with the Kaiserin-Auguste-Viktoria Gymnasium in Celle which led to many happy exchange visits between the pupils of both schools, culminating in a highly acclaimed performance of *Hamlet* in Celle in 1980 as part of their school's 175th birthday celebrations: they hope to join

'Dame Alice' in celebrating its centenary.

Miss Forster wrote in September 1953: 'As I write, I have by me letters from girls staying with their friends in Germany. I was delighted to receive these, which remind me of our contacts with other nations. We are glad to have in school members of staff from France, Belgium and Germany, and girls of various nationalities. We welcomed some fifteen girls from Celle at the beginning of the Summer term, and have had visits from French and Norwegian girls too. A party visited Paris at Easter and others have been to various parts of France and Norway. We receive the magazine of a school in Malaya and correspond with some of the pupils. We all hope that in these and other ways firm friendships may be established such as I have made with the Head of the school at Rheydt in the Rhineland.' Later years have seen the fulfilment of these hopes, as the daughters of Old Girls follow in their mothers' footsteps, in many cases continuing a family friendship begun in these years.

The end of School Guides

The School Guide companies disappeared in the late 1940s, the last report of their activities appearing in *Uisage* 1947. Two companies had continued throughout the war – they had formed a guard of honour on the occasion of the visit of Queen Marie of Yugoslavia to the school in 1942, and in 1946 helped to line the route in St. Paul's Square when H.R.H. Princess Elizabeth (now H.M. the Queen) visited Bedford. In the latter year, lack of support led to the amalgamation of the two companies, and then to their disappearance in 1947–48.

The Ranger Company founded in 1943, later met the same fate. Probably the increased academic pressures together with the fact that a much larger percentage of girls lived outside Bedford and thus had travelling problems contributed to their cessation. Nevertheless many girls and Old Girls have maintained an interest in Guiding up to the present time, serving in companies in their own localities.

The School Council

Miss Forster's strong belief that training in democratic principles should form part of girls' education resulted in the formation of a School Council at the beginning of the Autumn term 1946. Its composition and purpose were clearly outlined by its first secretary: 'Its members consist of form captains from forms I to V, school captains and representatives of the staff. Subjects discussed are those which concern the general welfare and organisation of school life and activities. Proposals for discussion by the Council can be made by any members of the school through their form representative. These proposals are first read at assembly so they may be discussed by the whole school in form-time. Comments are then passed on to the Council by the form representatives, after which the proposals are voted upon, the staff having the power of veto. A restricted number of visitors, consisting of one girl from each form, is also invited to attend Council meetings which are held once every three weeks, but do not take part in the proceedings. In this way all members of the school by offering suggestion and criticism, may take some part in shaping the life of the school according to its changing needs. It has the added value of familiarising members and visitors with the routine of a public meeting and trains them in the power of expressing coherent opinions in public.

'The most important outcome of the activities of the School Council has been the adoption of a school uniform. A gardening club has also been formed and it is hoped that a Ballroom Dancing class will be arranged during the winter terms. Regulations forbidding visits to the cinema during term-time have been relaxed for members of the IV, V and VI forms at the weekends, and a scheme for sending representatives of the school on visits abroad during the holidays is still under discussion.

'Some criticisms of the constitution and methods of the Council are that the VI form make up too large a proportion of members, that proposals are sometimes irrelevant and unsuitable for discussion by the Council, and that the time allotted for Council meetings is too short. It is hoped that these criticisms may be discussed and any faults righted this term.' (from *Uisage* 1947)

Various subjects were aired during further meetings: film and film-strip projectors were requested later in 1947 though they were not able to be purchased until 1950. Corridor problems were dicussed, and it was decided to impose silence to help speed up the traffic. This was so successful that the following meeting extended the rule to the cloakroom at 1.55 p.m., but by October 1950 the 'corridor' question was under discussion again, and it was decided to abandon the 'silence' rule, and impose one of 'single file' instead. The cry of 'Single file in the corridors, please' remained a very familiar one for many subsequent years. In 1951 the subject of Guild collections arose: should forms choose their own charities instead of giving all money to school charity choices – and after discussion it was agreed that forms should be allowed to make a choice, but that the whole school should give to each in turn. The Honours Roll, signed by school and form captains for many years, was another suggestion as was also the Cricket Club, while in 1952 came the beginning of House drama and music competitions, a School Council decision 'to help to promote House spirit'. Regular meetings have not continued but the Council has met since when occasion required.

It is interesting to note that in these years the enforcement of discipline was felt necessary and requested: in 1955 Disorder marks or Discipline marks were proposed while in the following year when the 'Lock-up' rules and 'exeats' were discussed, the general opinion was that these things were still necessary, indeed 'a useful function of school life.'

Uniform

After the exigencies of the war years there seemd an almost universal desire to return to uniform, though, of course, there was much discussion over detail. The result for winter was a return to the white square-necked blouses, introduced in the twenties, worn with a navy tunic with a plain top and slightly flared skirt instead of the pleated tunics of the pre-war period. The belt showed one of the five house colours replacing the coloured bar brooch. A blue belt indicated junior games colours: senior colours entitled the wearing of blue girdles, or 'tails' as they were popularly known. Out of doors, navy gaberdine rain coats or winter coats were worn, and navy felt hats with plain cornflower blue hat-bands showing the school badge at the front: a navy blue beret, to be worn so that the badge showed, was an optional extra preferred by many. Many, too, are the memories connected with the wearing of the beret depending on the prevailing fashion, from wearing it on the back of the head, rather like a plate, when it had to be fastened on with hair clips, to the later fashion when bouffant hair styles almost hid the beret from view and necessitated the war-cry of 'Show the badge!' (They also made excellent 'skimmers' and met with unfortunate accidents on buses.)

Dresses for the summer were candy striped with a colour choice of red, green, navy or brown. The style for the younger girls had a gathered waist and Peter Pan collar, and for the older girls an open neck, and a gored skirt; both styles had a self-belt with stripes lengthways, or they could be worn with a narrow white belt with a buckle. A navy blazer with the D.A.H.S. badge (showing the house colour) was worn with a Panama hat or a beret out-of-doors.

In the Summer term of 1952, 'prefects began to wear their distinctive uniform of swathed striped hat bands, striped ties and blazers in school blue', while the following term the 'new blue pullovers in the school colour added a brighter note to the winter uniform.'

Other activities

While self-government was being fostered by the School Council, the School branch of C.E.W.C. with Miss Broadway's inspiration, was increasing its knowledge of world affairs. By 1955 both senior and junior branches were thriving and some senior members attended the Christmas Holiday Lectures at the Central Hall, Westminster from 1953 onwards. The Debating Society, too, which began in 1949, and flourished thereafter, grew 'out of the enthusiasm of last year's IVc for expressing views and challenging other forms to discuss them. . . . The Society has developed an atmosphere in which no one is afraid to stand up and express her ideas and we have all noticed how each one of us has developed a fluent and unhesitating way of expressing herself with hardly any "hums!", "ahs!" and "wells!".' The first joint debate was held with the Bedford High School in July 1949, and joint debates with the staff were thoroughly enjoyed by all.

Drama

Other clubs came and went as enthusiasm waxed and waned,

but the already strong dramatic traditions gained a permanent outlet in the newly formed Drama clubs. In the early years drama had provided part, often a major part, of each Speech Day programme, and staff and girls, combined and separately, used their talents to entertain and raise money for worthy causes, both very successfully: many of these have already been mentioned. Forms each put on their own performances for end-of-term celebrations. Nor were the performances confined to the English language. In 1937 for example, each French division prepared and acted a French play which was reviewed in *Uisage*, while IV Upper A also demonstrated their talent in German.

Miss Cranmer remembers the Staff performing many one-act and longer plays in the 'new' hall in the playground at St. Paul's Square, including 'a riotous version of a silent film entitled *Love in the Desert*, with Miss Morris as a Charlie Chaplin hero, and Miss Foster as his faithful companion, while Mrs Long provided suitable accompaniment on the piano, and a disembodied voice announced the captions.'

Though the war deterred large scale dramatic efforts, activity continued and Miss Holmes' Elocution classes which were begun in 1941 provided an organised outlet and extra-training for their supporters. Perhaps the highlight of combined endeavour of staff and girls was *Twelfth Night* in March 1945 which raised £91 3s 8d for the Yugoslavia Emergency Fund. (School dinners at this time were 6d. (2½p) per day, fees were £12 a year, the total Guild of Help collections for 1944 came to £67 17s 2d.)

1946 saw the resumption of those expeditions which had been enjoyed before the war – to Stratford for *Macbeth*, to Oxford for a performance of *The Winter's Tale* in the garden of Exeter College, to Cambridge for *As You Like It*, a London visit to the New Theatre to see *Henry IV Part I*. 'Laurence Olivier's "Hotspur" was a wonderful example of speed in delivery, fine diction, and characterisation. Ralph Richardson's "Falstaff" was afterwards reported as the finest in living memory.' Many of these expeditions were to become annual events, while the range widened to include T. S. Eliot's *Murder in the Cathedral*, Shaw's *St. Joan*, and *Cyrano de Bergerac* in 1947–48, and Sophocles' *Oedipus Tyrannus* translated from the Greek and produced by Dr J. T. Sheppard.

The coming of the French players in November 1948, with *Les Précieuses Ridicules* by Molière and *L'Anglais tel qu'on Parle* by Bernard, were found to be both dramatically enjoyable by seniors of all the Bedford secondary schools ('even if they could not understand the French, they could guess what was happening by the actions of the players which were very good indeed') and 'very helpful, for luckily we have *Les Précieuses Ridicules* as one of our set books in the Higher School Certificate.' Further performances in subsequent years proved equally enjoyable.

For the school in general, however, drama came to life with the visits of the Compass Players, the first being in November 1949. 'The Compass Players' were founded in 1944 by John Crockett to help in creating a living theatre which could belong to the smaller communities as well as to the towns. Their impact was immediate: 'In the afternoon they performed John Crockett's version of *The Pardoner's Tale* before the school. One of the most thrilling scenes was the meeting of the three young rioters with a feeble old man, well described as being at "Death's door . . ." He wore a hideous mask, and his quavering voice was most effective. After the three young men had departed, the old man took the stage alone. He turned his back to the audience and drew his black cloak closer to him. We saw a skeleton-like hand come over the shoulder, grip the cloak, and return the way it came. This was one of the play's best moments. . . .'

The following November the school saw Marlowe's *Dr Faustus*: 'Being a travelling company, the players used no elaborate scenery, but based all the settings upon a pair of plain beige screens. . . . In the afternoon performance especially, the possibilities of lighting and music were exploited to the full – *Dr Faustus*, based on the Elizabethan conception of Black Magic, is not an easy play to "get over" to an audience of sceptical schoolgirls. Yet the dark flickering shadows, the sudden sheet lightning followed by the dull muttering notes of the storm, the urgent whispering of the voices of Conscience and Ambition, the melodious strains that summoned Helen from the Shades, the grotesque grace of the spirit dancers – all these combined to enlist our sympathies for the doomed Faustus. . . .'

On both these occasions evening performances were given to parents and to the general public.

In 1951 The Young Vic Company came to Bedford and a party was taken to see a performance of *The Merchant of Venice*, and again for many girls it was the first time they had seen a Shakespearean play performed by professional actors.

By this time the former Elocution Class had been replaced by Drama clubs, the first under Miss Cranmer's direction, and then under Miss Helliwell and Miss M. Holmes. Divided into groups for 'reading' as well as 'acting' it expanded rapidly, its first full-scale production, *Pygmalion* taking place in May 1952, followed by *Arms and the Man* 1953, with two shorter works *Thread o'Scarlet* by J. J. Bell, and the opening and closing acts of *Emma* adapted from Jane Austen's novel by Gordon Glennon in 1954. Though as was pointed out, the standards of production were not yet those of public performances, the idea of a school play was mooted, and also a combined reading with Bedford School Dramatic Club, which latter, however, had to be postponed owing to difficulties in arranging a suitable time.

Current events

The dramas of the world at large passed un-noted by most in the school. The two days' holiday given for Princess Elizabeth's wedding in 1947 was noted: it was closely followed in Miss Forster's 'Log' by mention of a talk on 'Gas and Electricity economy', while a reference is made in *Uisage* to the 'coupon-free' costumes in the plays of these years – clothes rationing did not end until 1949. The partition of India, the Berlin Airlift of the following year, the war in Korea are un-noted, though doubtless they formed the subjects of discussion in VI form groups and C.E.W.C. meetings. The general election of 1951 was preceded by a mock-election at school in 1950: each political party in the area sent a representative to school to explain its policy and girls were later chosen as candidates, but in school, 1951 was 'Festival Year'. Two parties, IIIB and the VI form, visited the Festival of Britain, bringing back many lasting memories, while the Old Girls had their Festival Weekend in July.

The nation as a whole, however, was soon preoccupied with the increasing ill-health of the King. 'I vividly remember the general anxiety felt when we saw in the newspapers the picture of the King and Queen waving goodbye to Princess Elizabeth and the Duke of Edinburgh on the start of their tour. The King looked so ill. . . . The whole school was summoned into the Hall to hear the news of his death: it was a very awesome moment.'

Several members of staff queued to pay their last homage at the lying-in-state in Westminster Hall; the chill winds and overcast skies but echoed the sorrow of all who waited. Representatives of staff and girls attended the memorial service at St. Paul's, Bedford. Mourning was transmuted into thanksgiving 'for the example he set of unwearied devotion to duty: for his steadfast courage in years of war and manifold anxieties: for the love and loyalty borne to him by a great family of peoples in all parts of the world,' and thanksgiving merged almost imperceptibly into hope for the future as we sang 'God save the Queen'. A new Elizabethan age had begun.

'Thanksgiving' and 'dedication' were the keynotes when on 13th June 1952 all who enjoyed the benefits of the Harpur Endowment joined with the Mayor and Corporation of Bedford in a service to commemorate the four hundredth anniversary of the granting by Edward VI of Letters Patent to the Mayor and Corporation of Bedford for the endowing of a school. Only the inspiration of the service could be carried back to everyday routine, to remind us that we each had our individual work 'preparing ourselves for the larger tasks ahead. . . . with courage and resolution dedicating our own personal gifts to the love and service of man.'

The events of Coronation Year echoed this theme – from the 'Coronation Lecture' given at school by Dr Perkins, sacrist at Westminster Abbey, to the Coronation itself in which all shared, some as part of the crowds in London itself, or as viewers or listeners in countless homes: television came into its own on that day as viewers shared both in the solemnity of the service in the Abbey and Queen Salote's fine disregard for the rain as she drove back to the Palace in an open carriage. The announcement on Coronation Day of the conquest of Everest by a team representative of the Commonwealth was an additional inspiration.

Even the losses served as a reminder: Queen Mary's death after a life of service to the nation, and that of Miss Tonkin, who in her sphere served her generation, and is likewise remembered with thanksgiving.

Miss Forster's contribution to school music

When Miss Forster first came as Headmistress she had expressed her intention of extending and enriching the musical work of the school, and it was soon possible to see her hand at work organising and making full use of existing talent as well as bringing in new. One of her first appointments was that of Mr Freyhan, an additional music teacher 'so that classes could be taught separately, making possible the study of sight singing, theory and appreciation of music'. He joined Miss Huntington, who had taught singing part-time since 1917 and had achieved incredibly high standards in singing, considering the usual size of the classes was between 50 and 60 girls.

Audrey Armstrong (*née* Mathers) used to look forward to the 'weekly singing lessons, the only musical activity of a regular nature in the school curriculum', with Miss Huntington 'who taught us to produce our voices properly, to breathe as singers should, but above all to enjoy learning to sing a wide variety of music, mostly in two or three part form'. A choir had competed regularly in the Bedfordshire Eisteddfod, as the present Musical Festival was then called, and from 1926 onwards each form, and after the house system came into being, each house, competed in an Annual Singing Competition for the Rose bowl 'Hunty' presented.

By the end of the war the annual Carol Concerts with the Boys' Modern School had been established, and 50 girls had taken part in Vaughan Williams' *Thanksgiving for Victory Anthem* recorded in November 1944 and broadcast on Victory Day. Every Speech Day was marked by a full and varied choral programme, but it was not until Miss Pace was appointed as Head of the new Music Department in 1949 that choral work on a larger and more formal scale came into being, and it also became possible to offer music as an optional external examination subject.

Since no instrumental music was taught in school an orchestra was much harder to maintain than a choir. Nevertheless there were usually some members of staff who could play and Miss Buckley was able to utilise such talent as was available for special occasions. Miss Carter has some lively memories of practices under Miss Buckley's baton (a ruler!). Miss Tonkin noted in her 1932 Report that the School Orchestra had been revived with Miss Maud Freeman, L.R.A.M., an Old Girl, as conductor, but little is recorded of its activities. At one time in the late thirties the 'Pipe Class' met regularly and did 'some very advanced work' under Miss Huntington's direction and supported by her 'unflagging energy'.

Instrumental music lessons

In 1947, however, came the beginning of instrumental music lessons in school with Miss R. Rapaport's violin lessons to individuals and small groups after school. Thereafter, progress is noted every year by Miss Forster in her annual Reports to the Governors. In 1948 a small orchestra was started: the *Uisage* report gives a little more detail. 'The Orchestra was formed in the Spring term. It consists of five first violins, three second violins, one viola and three 'cellos; these, together with the conductor, Miss Rapaport, and the pianist, Marilyn Collyer, make fourteen members altogether.' (Miss Forster noted the need of a double bass.)

The following year Miss B. Van der Straaten, L.R.A.M., an Old Girl, came in to give some individual 'cello lessons, and this year saw the beginning of the summer concerts which have been enjoyed for so many years since. In 1950 a new double bass was purchased, and the following year a full size grand piano, while the Instrument Fund was started so that it would be possible to buy wind and string instruments to lend to girls who could not yet afford their own. Mr John Davies came one day a week to teach wind instruments and Mrs Else Cross to teach piano, and by September 1951 the numbers of those learning an instrument in school were: thirty-one, the piano; twenty-one, the violin; three, the viola; three, the 'cello; four, the clarinet; one, the flute and one the oboe. With such rapid expansion, and under the expert tuition of the music staff, both choirs and orchestras made good progress and 1951 saw their performance of Pergolesi's *Stabat Mater* with soloists from the Guildhall School of Music. The first orchestra, too, entered the North London Music Festival for the first time and was awarded first place, winning high praise from the adjudicator, who added 'This orchestra means business'.

Though the orchestras made their music for all to hear, rehearsing in the Hall and music room in the dinner hours, it was difficult to find rooms in the school for all the instrumental lessons: first, a small room was made on the ground floor in Dame Alice House by cutting off one end of a storeroom, and not until the Summer term of 1952 was it possible to use the Abbey. From then on music remained a constant background for those in the dining rooms below, while more polished performances were enjoyed on Speech Day, and at Christmas, usually as part of the Christmas celebrations, as well as the summer concerts. The House Music competition, held biennially, made its first appearance in 1952 so that the musically talented could contribute to their House achievements as well as enjoy the internal competition.

Externally the first orchestra maintained its high standards, gaining the prize in their class in the Bedfordshire Music Festival as well as gaining another first in the London Music Festival, while they also played at the U.N.O. Concert, performing Bach's *F. Minor Piano Concerto* with Miss Ruth Harte as soloist. On the latter occasion they were supported by the senior choir, who sang Moeran's *Commendation of Music*, (sung previously at the Bedfordshire Music Festival with the set song *The Manx Spinning Song* when they had been placed second, three marks behind the winners), *The New Commonwealth*, by Vaughan Williams, and his arrangement of two folk songs, *My Father left me an acre of land* and *The Green Meadow*. The choir and orchestra combined again in the Autumn term 1952 in the production of Bach's *Christmas Oratorio*, which, with Stella Ruthven and Gillian Tebbutt as soloists, was performed on Speech Day and again at the Christmas concert.

The good foundations laid in these early years led on to further development and expansion which needed more staff, both full and part-time. The personal touch comes with Miss Rapaport's early memories of the orchestra in *Uisage* 1955.

The orchestra

'It is with more than a streak of nostalgia that my mind goes back to those remote and glowing autumn days of 1947, and to that first small group of violinists who had their lesson in the

Hall on Saturday mornings. Those seem far-off days when singly or in small classes we learned and struggled together – when all shapes and sizes of us were seized with the desire to play the violin and to overcome the countless obstacles that elusive instrument places in the path of the beginner or experienced player alike. . . .

'When we had learned to draw a straight bow across the strings and had begun to use our fingers, in that very first term the School Orchestra was founded. We were a small gathering, but perhaps our enthusiasm has never reached the peak of those early days. Miss Forster and Miss Carter were our backbone, with Miss Reichsmann and her newly acquired skill as a viola player. As I write this, I can still feel exactly that mingled sense of fascination and horror when one day Miss Reichsmann strode into orchestra (it was a very cold day) and said, "It is very stuffy here, girls – open all the windows!" to be followed a moment later by Miss Forster and her 'cello, whose entry was cut by an icy blast with music flying in all directions, and the merciful and irresistible "Girls, it is far too cold and windy here, close all the windows!"

'It is a far cry from Adam Carse's *Lullaby and Dance* (our first piece) to the *Carnival of the Animals*, the *St. Paul's Suite*, the *3rd Brandenburg Concerto* or the Pergolesi *Stabat Mater*, and we travelled over many stony inclines to reach those heights. Frequently we rehearsed to an inquisitive audience on the terrace with flattened, whitened noses pressed to the french windows!

'Gradually new members joined us – Miss Helliwell, followed by other 'cellists, Miss Pace, first as a powerful violinist and then as a still more powerful viola player – Mrs Long, invaluable on the double bass (an instrument without which no orchestra, however small, can call itself complete), Miss Whysall and many more violinists, Miss Key, with her viola and a few brave girls who changed over to this instrument; clarinettists, flautists, and finally, because we still lacked an oboe, Miss Forster took lessons and divided herself between the oboe and the 'cello. All the time there was a waiting list of violinists and consequently the Second Orchestra was formed – partly because we might have spilled over the edges of the platform, and also because we felt we must keep up the standard we had forged for ourselves, and a second orchestra, whilst obtaining training and achievement in its own right, also provided us with players as we needed them and as they became sufficiently proficient. . . .

'Of all the leaders that the orchestra has had since its formation, none, I think, has filled me with greater awe than Janet, who could be relied upon utterly to see that sectional rehearsals well and truly took place during the week! Some concerto performances I look back on with pleasure; Monica in the Bach *F Minor Piano Concerto*, the four girls who so ably tackled the *Carnival of the Animals* in turns, and performances by different violinists of the Bach *Double Concerto*, the Vivaldi *A Minor*, and other works. We had good leaders, too, for some of our Chamber Music classes; I recall especially Jean with her group in the early Mozart *G Major Quartet*, and Janet with her players in the Schumann *Piano Quintet*. . . .'

Recitals

As well as being teachers the visiting music staff were also performers of distinction. Their first recital in November 1951, given in aid of the Instruments Fund, was much appreciated by their audience and contributed greatly to the growing appreciation of music in the school at large and among parents and friends. Miss Pace, perhaps, expressed the general feeling, when reporting the recital given by Miss Rapaport, Mr Davies and Mrs Cross in November 1953, she referred to them as 'what we affectionately regard as our own Trio' – they shared their skill and enjoyment of music with us all and it became part of our heritage.

Added to these were the concerts given by visiting musicians: Kathleen Long's piano recital in 1946, Leon Goossen's oboe the following year: folk songs by Eve Maxwell Lyte in 'a long dress of green velvet with lace collar and cuffs' in 1948. Benjamin Britten with Peter Pears was to have come in 1949, but he was ill and his place was taken by Bruce Boyce, baritone, with Gerald Moore as his accompanist: his *Modern American* songs gave much pleasure to the younger members of the audience. In subsequent years we enjoyed folk songs well presented by Peggy Stack, the skilled performance of the Robert Masters Pianoforte

Quartet, and two recitals given by Andrew and Robin McGee, youthful but accomplished performers on violin and piano. The school year 1952–53 brought three very memorable recitals: Florence Hooton in the Autumn term, whose 'cello performance held her audience spellbound: the London Harpsichord Ensemble in the Spring term transporting us back to the eighteenth century with its music and enthralling us with the dainty sounds of the harpsichord. 'What I remember most clearly, however, was the recital given by Frederick Fuller, baritone, and Julian Bream, guitar. I had never realised before the full scope of the guitar as an instrument and Mr Bream, then aged eighteen, demonstrated his technical skill in his expressive solo playing, as well as providing a very satisfying accompaniment to Mr Fuller's songs. *Heidenröslein* and *El Tecolote* have left a particularly vivid memory.'

The last, but certainly not least of the recitals, took place in Miss Forster's final term, the Spring term 1955, and was that given by the Dennis Brain Ensemble which consisted of Gareth Morris, flute, Sidney Suffolk, oboe, Stephen Waters, clarinet, Cecil James, bassoon, Dennis Brain, horn, and Wilfrid Parry, piano. To hear such musicians was both an enjoyable and unforgettable experience and one greatly appreciated by the audience.

The development of the musical work and the appreciation of music by the school was perhaps Miss Forster's most memorable contribution as Headmistress, but she was also active in many other ways.

Miss Forster's other activities

The Parent-Teacher Association, formed in the autumn of 1946 to take the place of the Parents' Association, dormant during the war years, owed much to her energies. By 1948, membership numbers had risen to 400 families, and the termly meetings, as well as social events, included talks such as that by Mr Lucking on 'Grammar Schools and their problems', shorter talks by members of staff on their subjects and a Brains Trust, while the P.T.A. sponsored some of the musical recitals, and dramatic performances such as those given by the Compass Players.

The Old Girls' Association, too, was grateful for her unfailing support: the combining of the O.G. leaflet with the school magazine to strengthen the link between Old and present girls, the O.G. Choir, the O.G. Drama Club, the annual party given for the blind were among her suggestions. The Buckley Memorial Prize for History was instituted, and also an annual scholarship for music to one of the pupils of the school, while the O.G.A. shared in the furnishing of the Tonkin room, providing reading racks to be used for periodicals.

The establishment of the Boarding House in 1950 was another result of Miss Forster's energetic concern, also the re-organisation of the house system in 1952 when the five houses were replaced by six, three 'town' houses and three 'country', and the 'saints' became Beagley, Humphriss, Gillions (for three of the girls present in the early days of the school), Porter, Dolby and Tonkin (for the three past Headmistresses). But perhaps her greatest memorial is to be found in the lives of Old Girls who consciously or unconsciously absorbed her teaching; her insistence on good standards of behaviour, her honesty and straightforward way of going to the point and not evading the issue, however unpleasant it might be; her keenness to see every girl make the best of her talents and opportunities and her untiring efforts to help those in personal difficulties.

Her 'retirement'

Her retirement was in name only. When she died in October 1968 a correspondent wrote to *The Times*: 'Miss Irene L. Forster, who died on October 8th at her home in London, was a pioneer in the education of musically talented children. She was 66.

'Her mother was one of the earliest students at the Royal College of Music, and she herself was a good amateur 'cellist. From her experiences as assistant at Princess Mary High School, Halifax, and Haberdashers' Aske's, Acton, and as Headmistress of the Girls' High School, Wellington and The Dame Alice Harpur School, Bedford, she came to realise that special provision for children with an exceptional aptitude for musical performance and composition was essential and must be offered in line with the educational opportunities in this field of most eastern European countries.

'She therefore retired young from conventional school headship and, in January 1962, helped to found and agreed to become Principal of the Central Tutorial School for Young Musicians. This was a pioneer venture, the first in this country to offer a first-class general education with special facilities for children with strong musical potential. She gave generously, both of herself and of her financial resources and, in spite of considerable suffering during these last months, she was in office until ten days before her death.

'This country should feel greatly indebted to her, not only for the flourishing school of which she was principal but for her inspiration and leadership which has encouraged the launching of other schemes, and at least one other school of a similar kind outside London.'

Building and Reconstruction

Miss Lawson Brown

Miss Forster's successor was Miss H. Lawson Brown, a classicist with an Oxford M.A. degree, who after teaching experience in various parts of the country had in 1947 become Headmistress of Edgehill College, Bideford, a Direct Grant School of 380 girls. When she came to The Dame Alice Harpur School in 1955 she brought an enthusiasm and a great capacity for work which was to find good outlet and last throughout her tenure of office.

The 75th birthday

One of the first major events celebrated was that of the school's 75th birthday in 1957, marked by the visit of H.R.H. The Duchess of Gloucester on 8th May, the Commemoration Service in St. Paul's Church, and the Pageant. Each of these brings back many memories – the cold greyness of the weather on 8th May – the excitement of the Duchess' arrival – the impressive silence and uniform blue colour of the gymnastics display contrasted with the lively piano music and the brightly coloured national dress of the dancers – the new school flag flying in the breeze; the spring green of the trees on the Embankment as long lines of girls made their way to St.Paul's – the combined choirs' anthem *I waited for the Lord* – the address given by the Bishop of Gloucester stressing our link with the past, and our responsibility to God for service in the future: the 'scenes' of the pageant from the past and looking forward, concluding with Sir William Harpur's vision of his work and its great future – his words 'My purpose shines the fairer for the years' – the heartfelt singing of *Non Nobis, Domine.*

Early expansion

At this time the school was ready for expansion. It had successfully absorbed the greater numbers of the 1940s and was beginning to achieve good academic standards in the new G.C.E. examinations. In 1951, the first year of these examinations, with a subject entry of 272 at Ordinary level the pass rate was 78 per cent: at Advanced level the total subject entry was 41, and the pass rate 83 per cent. By 1955 subject entries at O level had increased to 491, with an 85.5 per cent pass rate, and at A level with a subject entry of 61, the pass rate was 82 per cent. Seven girls had gained State Scholarships during this period. The provision of the houses in Cardington Road meant that more space was now available and could be effectively utilized, while the teaching staff had been strengthened numerically to cope with the increased numbers.

Selections from Reports give an interesting summary of progress in the ensuing years.

In 1955 'the Preparatory Department, now in Kilpin House (No. 48) has been increased to three forms, one for each year group, 7–9 years, plus IR (the ten-year-old group) which is included in the senior school for the purposes of the Direct Grant.'

1956 saw a four stream entry in the first year for the first time: in the following September each year was divided into four forms except for the VI form which, now numbering 100, was divided into five groups.

Wing House (No. 46) was ready for the VI form in 1956: in addition to the Tonkin Room there were three classrooms, a Modern Languages room, cloakroom space for 50–60 girls, and a staff cloakroom.

In 1957, in the main building, the Studio, Studio annexe and store were converted into a Physics laboratory, an Advanced Chemistry laboratory and a dark room. The Studios were transferred to Dame Alice House, which was itself altered to provide an additional cloakroom, a housecraft room, a new needlework room and store, a new music room and an additional form room.

The caretaker's flat in Kilpin was taken over – this gave a second music room, a staff room and an extra room for the Junior School. Another room was enlarged in the following year to take twenty-four seven-year-olds instead of seventeen.

In 1962, the flat at the rear of Wing House was absorbed and adapted to provide classrooms for two VI form groups, while the staff room extensions provided much needed space for the increased numbers of staff.

By this time, however, serious difficulties were arising in connection with the provision of mid-day meals in the Abbey. A total of 570 girls having dinner meant that there had to be three sittings for hot dinner, using the two dining rooms originally provided for the purpose, and also the entrance hall: in addition there were two sittings of cold lunch in a classroom, as there was no cold dinner room at all. There was the additional difficulty of taking the 'hot-dinner' queue across Duck Mill Lane at a time when traffic was comparatively heavy. From Miss Lawson Brown's request that the Governors would consider the urgent need for more dining space came a full review of the existing premises, and a formulation of a long-term plan of reconstruction and improvement.

The Douglas Gordon Building

This resulted in the provision of the Douglas Gordon Building, whose Foundation Stone was laid on 1st October 1965, and which was formally opened on 13th July 1967.

The Foundation Stone was laid by Lord Luke of Pavenham, son of Lady Luke, who had laid the Foundation Stone of the new School in June 1937. 'It was a memorable occasion for the School. Lord Luke, Sir Douglas Gordon, several of our governors and their wives; the architect, Mr Henry Inskip, and the foreman of the builders assembled on the platform and were welcomed by Miss Lawson Brown. Lord Luke in a short speech recalled the visit of his mother to the school and the gift made to her on that occasion of a glass goblet inscribed with a Coronation monogram. He said how pleased he was to be able to be with us for the ceremony of laying the foundation stone of the new building.

'The platform party then left the hall, in procession, preceded by the school prefects and form captains, and made their way to the building site. Here the architect presented Lord Luke with a silver trowel and mallet; the master mason spread cement on the bed, and the stone was slowly lowered into position. Lord Luke tapped the stone with the mallet three times and declared it "well and truly laid".'

In the ensuing months the whole school watched the progress of the new building with great interest, and looked forward to its completion. The death of Sir Douglas Gordon in September 1966 saddened all who knew him, especially those at the four schools who had benefited so much from his active interest and wise guidance as Chairman of the Governors of the Harpur Trust.

'There was no doubt in our minds as to the appropriateness of naming our splendid new building after Sir Douglas, and it was with pride and satisfaction that we gathered on 13th July 1967, for the formal opening of the Douglas Gordon Building.

'Against the background of trees and lawns and the new rose garden, the school assembled on a hot, sunny day, in front of the impressive terrace where an awning had been erected at the opening to the new Entrance Hall. Senior prefects escorted visitors – many of them "old girls" and former members of staff – to their seats and then the platform party – Sir John Howard, Mrs Christopher Soames, Lady Douglas Gordon, Mrs Helen McInnes, Major S. Whitbread, Canon J. H. King, Mr Henry Inskip and Miss Lawson Brown – took their places.

'Sir John Howard, Chairman of the Governors of the Harpur Trust, spoke first, emphasising the importance of the day's proceedings. Miss Lawson Brown welcomed all our distinguished visitors and referred to the speed and efficiency with which the builders had worked to complete the buildings. She said how glad she was that Mrs Christopher Soames had consented to be our Guest of Honour, for her connection with the school had been a long and happy one. Mrs Soames then made her speech, saying how pleased she was to be with us on this important occasion and mentioning her many links with Miss Lawson Brown herself, and with the school.

'The architect, Mr Henry Inskip, then presented the Ceremonial Key to Mrs Soames and she opened the door, thus symbolically declaring the extensions officially open. Escorted by Miss Lawson Brown and Sir John Howard, she stepped inside the Entrance Hall and unveiled the memorial plaque to Sir Douglas Gordon. Canon J. H. King offered a prayer of dedication and then Mrs Helen McInnes, Sir Douglas' daughter, unveiled the photographic portrait of Sir Douglas which hangs just inside the Hall. Major Whitbread moved a vote of thanks to the Guest of Honour, the assembled company sang a hymn, and the formal part of the proceedings was over.

'While the main part of the school went home, the sixth form escorted visitors round the new building where, in every subject room, there was an exhibition. These exhibitions, in the Mathematics, Geography, History, Needlework, Art and Domestic Science rooms and in the Biology laboratory, represented the work of the departments concerned and provided a great variety of fascinating material for inspection. . . . The new buildings and the converted sixth form house were open to parents for the entire evening, and a constant stream of fresh visitors enjoyed looking at the exhibitions and marvelling at the splendour of the sixth form Common Room.'

The new Sixth Form House

The availability of the Douglas Gordon Building made possible major alterations in other buildings. Dame Alice House now became the Sixth Form House: the former Art, Needlework and Cookery rooms became seven Tutorial Rooms and four large Study Centres, while the Common Room referred to above occupied the front part of the first floor of Kilpin House. These changes were greatly appreciated by the members of the sixth form. Elizabeth Fisher, then Head Girl, and Lesley Bebb reported in *Uisage*:

'The study centres provide a quiet atmosphere for work and those requiring relaxation are now able to take advantage of the comfortable Common Room. These different surroundings have led to a new way of life for the Sixth Former. We have formed a smaller unit within the community without losing touch with life in the main school.

'In the Sixth Form House, work continues in an atmosphere similar to that of a college. Lessons in the Tutorial Rooms are informal, and private study is carried out in the quiet of the Study Centres. . . .

'The Common Room was opened at the beginning of this year – and has never been empty since! Its modern décor and comfortable furniture provide ideal conditions for relaxation. In the small, well-equipped kitchen, hot or cold drinks can be made, and meals can be cooked by those who are staying at school for extra-curricular activities. A variety of magazines provide a happy contrast to normal scholi stic literature. . . . We feel that sixth form life has improved greatly as a result of these innovations. . . .'

The Sixth Form House remained the home of the Careers Room except for a few weeks when the house was in the hands of the builders. With the new arrangements, the old Sixth Form Studio became a display centre for university and college prospectuses, careers pamphlets and books. Girls could use the room as a Reference Library for Careers, an extension to the section in the main library, while the Careers Room itself was used by Miss Dickson or Miss Durham for dealing with individual queries, discussions and interviews.

The Music House

The moving of the Sixth Form meant that the Prep. Department was able to move into Wing House, which was altered and renovated for them, while Kilpin House, which they vacated, became the Music House, providing two class singing rooms, four rooms for the teaching of instruments, a practising room, and also a speech-training room. The Sick Room, too, was transferred from Dame Alice House to a front room on the ground floor.

The Preparatory House

The passing of the 'Orchard', necessitated by the erection of the new building occasioned some regret: it had been used by the Preps. for so long and had given so much scope for imaginative play. *Uisage* 1961 contains an entry entitled 'Moving House in the Orchard' by Susan Hill of Prep. III.

'When we found three ants' nests in our old house, we thought we would like to move. We were scouting round the orchard, when we saw an opening between a house and a tree. That was a good place to have a house, because, if we liked, we could make people pay bricks if they wanted to go through the gap. So we set to work moving our house. We needed three people to move it, one to guard the old house, one to guard the new house, and one to carry bricks. When it came to carrying slabs of stone, two people would carry them. We had to move our tin of brick dust as well. We have it nearly half-full, partly through hard work, and partly through tricking the cake shop assistants. My friend and I would go to the cake shop, and I would ask how much a certain jar of brick dust was. My friend would overhear, and take the right sized brick from the shop. She would give it to me, and I would exchange it for the brick dust. So we would get it for nothing.

'There is a hollow near our new house, and we fill it with twigs, and lay dried grass on the top, so that some people who are not looking where they are going fall in. We charge them two quarters of an oblong brick, but as soon as the bricks are paid, we eagerly set to work to fill up the hollow again.

'So, on the whole, we are very pleased that we found those three ants' nests, and moved.'

The Abbey demolished

Another passing, in 1968, was that of the Abbey. With the new dining hall in use, and the music rooms in Kilpin House it was no longer needed, and the Harpur Trust had to consider its future. A report stated that the structural condition was so bad that renovation of the old building be very expensive, and although various suggestions were made it was clear that the heavy attacks of woodworm, dry rot and death-watch beetle put it beyond repair; at least a part of the building would have to come down. Opposition to this action was expected on the grounds that the Abbey was an important building of historic and architectural interest. In fact, however, study of the deeds showed that though some parts of the building were of the seventeenth century, extensive alterations had been made by various occupants, and much of the house dated from the nineteenth century.

The historical value of the building was therefore limited, and there was no effective opposition to its demolition. A new two-storey block of 24 almshouses – Harpur House – was erected on the site in 1970. The two entrance halls were finished with marble floor tiles recovered from the entrance of the old building, and in addition, the stained glass 'of some antiquity' from the East Window, was remounted in an illuminated screen in one of the entrance halls.

The Swimming Pool

Perhaps the most memorable of all the memorable events during these years, however, was the opening of the Swimming Pool in January 1970, both because so many had worked for it so long – staff, girls, Old Girls, parents and friends – and because of the day itself.

'After all the years of effort and perseverance it was with a great sense of pride that we at last heard splashes coming from our beautiful, brightly lit swimming pool in January of this year. It was, however, ironic that on the day chosen for the official opening ceremony a minor blizzard swept Bedfordshire. As reports of blocked roads and cancelled buses began to come in, we wondered rather dismally if, after all, we should be able to fit what remained of the school into a drastically diminished ceremony.

'All the girls who lived in the country areas – about half our total number – were sent home; those of us who remained just waited. We underestimated the courage and determination of our visitors. Undeterred, they battled their way through to us and when the ceremony was due to begin the platform was full of distinguished guests, among them Miss Lawson Brown's father and sister.

'Sir John Howard welcomed all the visitors and said what a proud day this was for the school and everyone connected with it. He reminded us how much this achievement owed to Miss Lawson Brown's foresight, determination and vision. He referred also to the generous gift of a steel diving board donated by Mrs Bollard in memory of her daughter Brenda, an Old Girl of the school, who died in 1962, aged twenty, after a brilliant start to her career.

'Guests, heads of departments, and representatives from the various forms in the school then moved to the pool itself where the official opening was to take place. The proceedings were relayed to those remaining in the hall.

'The highlights of the occasion were undoubtedly the unveiling of the two commemorative plaques – the main one which declares that the pool is the Lawson Brown Pool, and the other which records Mrs Bollard's gift. Perhaps the most delightful moment was when Ann Gellatly swam across the bath bearing aloft a bouquet which she presented in triumph to Miss Lawson Brown who, not unnaturally, had failed to notice this novel method of approach to her!

'Miss Lawson Brown, replying to Sir John Howard's tribute to her, declared that, proud as she was to have her family's name given to the pool, she felt very strongly that the pool represented the achievement of countless people – girls, Old Girls, parents, friends and governors. She particularly stressed how greatly indebted we were to the anonymous donor of £5,000 – a sum which brought our needed total to completion and which enabled us to have the pool not only finished but equipped.'

The new Boarding House

Miss Lawson Brown's final 'move' was that of the Boarding House. In the autumn of 1969 the Governors purchased Howard House, which with its extensive grounds and convenient situation adjacent to the main buildings made an ideal boarding house. It was prepared for occupation by the boarders during the Spring term of Miss Lawson Brown's last year, and opened for boarders on the first day of the Summer term.

Changing demands in curriculum

The provision of new buildings with their extra facilities could not but make organisation easier. It had become increasingly difficult to provide sufficient rooms for teaching, with four streams throughout the main school and a growing sixth form, together with the extra numbers of the 'bulge' noted particularly in the first and third forms in 1958.

More teaching space, particularly when the Douglas Gordon building was ready, meant, for example, that science studies for Ordinary Level could be developed to a really good pre-advanced level standard, encouraging more girls to study science in the sixth form. This was needed, both to meet the increasing interest in scientific knowledge and to satisfy the demand for science qualifications in the world at large. As a result the numbers of those studying Mathematics and Science grew steadily, both at Ordinary and at Advanced Levels, and good standards were maintained. The following figures can be given to show the tendency at Ordinary Level:

	1959	*1969*	*Pass rate 1969*
Number of girls offering O-level subjects	106	109	
Number of girls offering Mathematics	61	90	93%
Number of girls offering Physics	—	35	91%
Number of girls offering Chemistry	—	34	88%
Number of girls offering General Science	46	—	
Number of girls offering Biology	41	82	80%

The same trend can be observed at Advanced Level:

	1967	*1969*	*1971*	*Pass rate 1971*
Number of girls offering Mathematics	6	12	14	93%
Number of girls offering Physics	6	11	7	86%
Number of girls offering Chemistry	7	12	14	100%
Number of girls offering Biology	9	16	18	78%

Changes within the Mathematics department in these years owed much to Miss Southwell, its Head from 1953 to 1977. Her vision of the part Mathematics could play not only in a school curriculum but also in the lives of her students affected all who came into contact with her. While insisting on the highest possible standards of accuracy and presentation, her great concern was that the subject should be enjoyed at all levels. Under her leadership an entirely new syllabus was created – a careful amalgamation of traditional and modern Mathematics. The change from wholly traditional methods involved not only Miss Southwell but her entire department in a rigorous programme of lectures and courses. There was need for constant farsightedness and energy on Miss Southwell's part in reading up the new material and in preparing suitable exercises and worksheets in the absence of suitable textbooks. The new Mathematics room in the Douglas Gordon building gave an opportunity to create a centre which was a place where fascinating wall displays of mathematical shapes, curve stitching, apt quotations, interesting facts culled from newspapers and pictures and photographs of modern sculpture could be enjoyed, where the Mathematical Societies could explore fresh fields, as well as providing room for lessons.

The Needlework department was also able to expand with increased accommodation: the number of girls taking the Ordinary Level examination increased from 8 in 1957 to 23 in 1958, remaining fairly constant to 1969. Under the tuition of Miss Woodger, who had come to the school while it was still in St. Paul's Square in 1934 as Catering Supervisor, and became Head of Needlework later, girls became skilled both in dress-making and embroidery, as was seen in the Needlework exhibition at the opening of the Douglas Gordon building. Needlework was offered as a subject at Advanced Level, benefiting those who wished to take it up as a career, perhaps linked with Art and Design. In 1959, encouraged by Miss Woodger, all the girls who made dresses for their G.C.E. O-level examination, entered them for the Singer Sewing Machine Competition. Two girls reached the Regional Finals and one girl took her place with the 39 others from all parts of the British Isles in the Grand Finals held at Earls Court.

As well as re-appraisal and 'modernisation' of syllabuses within the departments, there was a marked expansion in the number of extra-curricular activities of these years. To the already established Games activities, Choirs and Orchestras, Debating Society, C.E.W.C., the Drama Clubs, the Film Society and the Natural History Society were added the Mathematical Societies, La Société Française, the History, Poetry and Arts Societies, Der Deutsche Klub, the Gardening and Floral Art Club, the Christian Union, La Sociedad Española (founded in 1969–70 when a Spanish O-level course for the sixth form was introduced) as well as some that had shorter lives.

Membership of these groups was not usually confined to seniors, though for effective organisation some had to be divided into age or year groups. The senior girls gained valuable experience helping to organise and run some of them with the guidance of staff, and all learned to contribute to the success of the whole by enthusiasm, helpfulness and regularity in attendance, so that in some respects they took the place of the 'house system' abandoned in 1958 'until further notice.' (It was revived in 1979 and there are at present four houses, Bunyan, Howard, Harpur and Russell.)

Another interesting feature in connection with these was the growth of inter-school activities. The first Inter-School Debate between the four Harpur Trust Schools took place in 1959; it became an annual event, growing to include nine schools, while joint debates with each of the three Harpur Trust schools were held regularly. Drama, too, profited greatly from co-operation with the boys' schools, and both the Drama Club and the French and German societies enjoyed play-readings with Bedford School and Bedford Modern School, while the school provided some actresses for Bedford Modern School's production of *The Winter's Tale* in February 1967. In 1965 the Senior Choir were invited by Bedford School to sing the gallery choir part in Britten's *St Nicholas Cantata* sung in the Great Hall with the Convent Choir and the Bedford School Choral Society. The S.C.M. conference was another occasion at which sixth form members from the four schools could meet for discussion, while in 1967 eight schools took part in the Geographical Association Inter-School Sixth Form quiz – won, after a close contest, by the Dame Alice team. The annual Sixth Form Dance might be mentioned in this connection though it had been held regularly since the end of the war, while the newly founded Sixth Form Scottish Dance Club maintained the link throughout the year.

A glimpse of the School Diary gives some idea of other activities – apart from lessons!

Spring Term 1967

23rd–25th February	Joint performance of *The Winter's Tale* with Bedford Modern School.
9th March	School team compete in Public Speaking Contest run by English Speaking Union.
11th March	School party to Wembley to Women's International Hockey Match.
13th March	VIth to *The White Devil* in Cambridge.
20th March	Senior Concert (including Pergolesi's *Stabat Mater*).

Easter Holidays

March–April	German girls from Celle – annual exchange visit.

28th March–11th April	School party to Sens, France.
23rd March–16th April	School party on cruise to Lisbon, Morocco and Corunna.
8th–18th March	School party to Italy. Rome and Venice with Miss Grigg, Miss Birtwhistle and Mrs Perry.
Summer Term	
12th May	VIth to *The Tempest* in Northampton.
22nd May	VIth move into reconstructed Dame Alice House.
25th May	Forms I–III to film *Henry V* at Granada.
4th July	VI_1 Geographers visit sand quarries at Leighton Buzzard and Woburn Sands with Geographical Association.
5th July	VI_1 Geographers visit Colworth House Farm, Sharnbrook.
6th–7th July	Fourth Form Geography Field Work days at Ivinghoe.
13th July	The Opening of the New Building.
17th July	VI_1 Geographers visit to Stewartby and the Brickworks.
19th July	The Bishop of Bedford visits the school.
20th–22nd July	*The Yeoman of the Guard* performed at the school.
Summer Holidays	
July	Party to Celle – annual exchange visit.
9th–16th September	Sixth Form Geography Field Course at Hackness, near Scarborough.
Autumn Term	
12th–18th October	Sixth form Ecology Course at Flatford Mill.
28th October	Sixth Form visit to performance of *Ghosts* in London.

2nd November	Careers Convention held in Dame Alice and Bedford Modern School.
11th November	Coffee evening at which prizes and certificates presented to girls who took public examinations in summer (held annually 1966 onward to replace Speech Day).
14th November	Sixth Form take part in Inter-School Quiz run by Geographical Association.
21st November	Literary and Debating Society visit Bedford School for joint debate.
6th December	McCall's Fashion Show held in school.
8th December	Sankt Niklaus Party in School. (German Department)

Miss Lawson Brown's retirement

Miss Lawson Brown's retirement in 1970 after fifteen years' service called forth many tributes. Past and present members of the sixth form appreciated their new facilities – the flexibility 'in which I, as a geographer, could acquire some knowledge of Science and Mathematics, yet still maintain my interests in things as diverse as French and Lacemaking' – the 'measure of trust with regard to our work which has been of inestimable help to me abroad and in Cambridge.' Others were 'impressed by the high standards and ideals which were presented to us by Miss Lawson Brown and her staff. . . . the happy and secure community in which I came to love and enjoy learning was entirely due to their help, encouragement and guidance.' Members of staff remembered 'her unwearied effort to maintain and raise standards of academic achievement and standards of self-discipline and community behaviour. Every aspect of school life – rules, uniform, meals, societies, examinations, holidays, prayers, groupings, subject choices – has come under scrutiny. Again and again she has sought to retain what is valuable and to dispense with anything which no longer serves a useful purpose. They remembered her loyalty and generous kindness to her "Old Staff" and their families, . . . the sympathy and help she gave unstintingly to those in trouble, her devotion to her family and her constant work for her church.' Her zest for, and obvious enjoyment of her work, seemed contagious, and in her relations with the Parent–Teacher Association and the Governors did much to make possible the achievements of these years.

Miss S. M. Morse, B.Sc., her successor, came to Bedford from Colston's Girls' School, Bristol, accepting the Headship at the time when the Harpur Trust was dealing with all the problems arising from the re-organisation of schools in Bedfordshire.

The Winds of Change

The last fifteen years have again seen changes in the pattern of education in the country at large. The constant renewal, adaptation and development within had been marked, but, just as in 1944 the school had adapted to the demands of '11+' and Direct Grant Grammar School standards, so it would have to meet the challenge of the demands expressed by the Government of 1965.

The passing of the 11+

'It is the Government's declared objective to end selection at eleven plus and to eliminate separatism in secondary education. The Government's policy has been endorsed by the House of Commons in a motion passed on 21st January, 1965:

"That this House, conscious of the need to raise educational standards at all levels, and regretting that the realisation of this objective is impeded by the separation of children into different types of secondary schools, notes with approval the efforts of local authorities to re-organise secondary education on comprehensive lines which will preserve all that is valuable in grammar school education for those children who now receive it and make it available to more children; recognises that the method and timing of such re-organisation should vary to meet local needs; and believes that the time is now ripe for a declaration of national policy." '

Under the Direct Grant Regulations, the L.E.A. were entitled to take up to 50 per cent of the annual entry to the Upper School (i.e. eleven upwards). In 1966 the L.E.A. had 68 per cent of the Upper School places at Bedford Modern School, and 78 per cent of the Upper School places at The Dame Alice Harpur School. It was obvious, then, that any implementation of the above policy would pose many difficult problems both for the L.E.A. and the Harpur Trust. Since the Governors of the Trust until 1974 included 'ex officio' the Mayor of Bedford, and the Members of Parliament for the County of Bedford, as well as twelve representatives appointed by the Local Authorities, six by the County Council, and six by the Bedford Town Council, there was no clear cut division between any of the bodies concerned and discussions continued freely throughout the last years of Miss Lawson Brown's term of office.

Reorganisation in Bedfordshire

By 1970, when Miss Morse arrived, the County Council as the Local Education Authority had declared their intention of introducing a 'Middle School' system of comprehensive education in Bedford and Bedfordshire on the basis of three stages – Lower (5–9 years), Middle (9–13 years) and Upper (13–18 years). At this time the L.E.A. entry into the school at 11+ was 71 and the total number of L.E.A. places was 519.

The Harpur Trust were anxious to co-operate and reach a working agreement with the County Council although the proposal raised problems of internal organisation, staffing and curriculum which would take time to resolve both in the Trust schools and in the L.E.A. schools. None of the Harpur Trust schools was equipped or staffed to take a fully comprehensive entry, but the Trust considered that the academic organisation of the schools could be adapted to receive pupils of a wider range of ability, provided the children were capable of profiting from the education provided by the school – that is, they should be able to take successfully a range of subjects in G.C.E. or C.S.E.

The 1971 agreement

The agreement reached in 1971 resulted in a reduced 11+ intake in 1973 (30+ girls instead of 60+ girls), and the first 13+ entry of 60 in 1974. As Miss Morse wrote in *Uisage* July 1974: 'The "shape" of our school will change year by year as we adjust to the new pattern. We now have four parallel forms for girls from the age of eleven years to fifteen years. Next year (i.e. September 1974) we shall have two parallel forms in Form I and we shall have six parallel forms in Form III: the 120 girls now in form

II will be joined by 60 new girls.'

Preparations had already been made for their reception, particularly with regard to the curriculum. (More teaching space would be needed in future years as the six parallel forms moved up and were divided into 'sets' but this was then only in the planning stage.) In the past, girls had begun a second foreign language, with a choice between Latin and German, at the beginning of the second form. From 1973 it was decided to delay the start until Form III, so that those new girls entering at this stage, and able to learn a second foreign language, could begin at the same time as girls already in the school. Until 1973 the third year timetable had included Cookery for all girls. With the revised arrangements for the Thirds extra time was given to Languages and Science, and Cookery not included in the timetable. If in the future, as was planned, an additional cookery room was added, then it would be possible to review the position. Instead Cookery was put into the timetable for Form II.

These were specific changes; more general change was outlined by Miss Morse to parents. C.S.E. courses were to be introduced in addition to O-level G.C.E. courses, and these could be followed by girls already in the school as well as those entering at 13+ who were not able to take a particular subject at O-level. These courses would be less demanding than an O-level course but would be interesting and valuable. Planning for these involved not only timetables, but preparation of new syllabuses, of textbook requirements, of lists of equipment needed for practical work, all made with a view to a second 13+ entry of 60 girls in 1975, and a planned increase to 100 in the following years. As Miss Morse said when originally outlining her plans, 'I suspect the future will be exciting, but exhausting from the point of view of planning. . . .'

Before this could happen, however, local government elections had led to a change of opinion within the L.E.A., and the decision was made to alter the 1971 agreement. Continuing discussions led to a decrease from the planned number of 100 in the 1976 and 1977 free place entry at 13+ to 75, and to 45 in the three following years. To these numbers each year 15 fee paying pupils were added to maintain full form groups of 30 in the Upper School. In 1981 no places were taken by the L.E.A.

Withdrawal of Direct Grant

The introduction of the 13+ entry was the result of only one aspect of Government policy. During these years the whole of the educational system was reviewed, particularly the part played by Public Schools, and, linked with this, the purpose of the Direct Grant system. In April 1975, after long and careful consideration of all the relevant factors, the Governors of the Harpur Trust decided that, in the event of the withdrawal of Direct Grant, both Bedford Modern School and The Dame Alice Harpur School should remain as Independent Schools, administered in accordance with the Trust scheme.

The withdrawal of Direct Grant finally became operative from September 1976. This meant, firstly, that all entrants from that date would have to pay higher fees – there would be no annual capitation grant, then £79, to supplement the fees paid, nor would the extra sixth form grant, then £84 a year, apply to them. Secondly, the exisiting fee remission scheme would no longer operate for them. The Governors had already passed a resolution 'to investigate the provision of assisted places for children of parents of limited means.' In 1976 they approved the use of the endowment of the Charity applicable to both Bedford Modern School and The Dame Alice Harpur School for a Bursary Scheme to provide for assisted places: in its first year a total of 72 Bursaries was provided at the two schools. 1981 saw the introduction of Government Assisted Places, and in September, although there were no Bedfordshire Free Place pupils, forty-four of the seventy-five Senior School entrants were awarded assistance with tuition fees either with a Harpur Bursary, or a Government Assisted Place.

Curriculum and reorganisation

The coming of independence had little effect on the curriculum or activities within the school. Pupils had been entered for C.S.E. for the first time in 1973, sixteen girls taking the examination in French, fourteen gaining Grade 1, and two Grade 2. By 1975 there were C.S.E. courses in French, German and Mathematics. Though candidates for the examination were mainly from form V, it was also taken by a few girls in the first year sixth who needed a grade one pass in Mathematics or a language. The following table gives a summary of examination results:

	C.S.E.			*G.C.E. O-level*		
	Subject entries	*Pass grade 1*	*2*	*Subject entries*	*Number of girls*	*Percentage success*
1976	39	23	10	857	116	85%
1977*	79	31	31	1,315	178	89%
1978	93	21	24	1,289	176	82%
1979	70	13	25	1,072	143	82%
1980	50	30	12	1,226	154	85%
1981	56	29	15	1,194	150	84%

*1977 was the first year that 13+ entrants took Public Examinations.

The greater numbers involved were catered for by the acquisition of the 'Vic Hallam' classrooms in 1976, which provided two general teaching rooms, and one for Art or Needlework, while room 5 became the eighth Science laboratory and the History room was divided to give a small extra division room. The following year part of one of the Physics laboratories was converted into an Optics room and a small Audio Visual technician's room, while the building of an extra store gave much needed storage space to the Physical Education department which had lost the Pavilion in 1970. In 1978 it was possible to meet staff needs by making room 23 into a study with an office for the Senior Mistress and the Second Mistress, while the Administrative Staff gained room 1 as office accommodation for the Bursar and his assistant, and a store. This did mean that some sixth form lessons were transferred to the Boarding House, and as a temporary measure the large tutorial room in the Sixth Form House was used for general teaching.

The graph – *The Growth of the Sixth Form 1955–81* – shows the general increase in its numbers in the seventies with marked annual fluctuations. The tendency of the seventies was for girls to stay for a full two-year course, rather than opting for the one-year course which had been more popular in the earlier years. The sharp rise in numbers in 1973 was in part caused by the transfer of twenty girls from St. Bede's (the Convent School) when their Sixth Form closed – thirteen more were transferred in 1974, and eleven in 1975. The first 13+ entrants reached the sixth form in 1977. Though there has been an obvious fluctuation in the number of subject entries at Advanced Level in the years 1974–81, the percentage pass rate has remained more or less constant at 88.5% or 89% – only in 1978 and 1980 did it fall below.

The increase in numbers since the Sixth Form House and the Common room came into being in 1967 has led to rather more crowded conditions, but the extra facilities are still much appreciated. Susan Rogers, looking back to the mid seventies from 1981, notes the relaxation of uniform rules – navy cardigans or jumpers instead of cornflower blue pullovers, the freedom of choice in suitable summer dresses, as well as a Sixth Form blazer and tie. Against this was set the increase in responsibility – both for the organisation and completion of their own work, and also for the general smooth running of the school, which, after the abolition of the prefect system in 1972 was shared by all members of the Sixth Form. She noted a change in the relationship between staff and girls – the recognition of their growing maturity – and appreciated the value of the Sixth Form

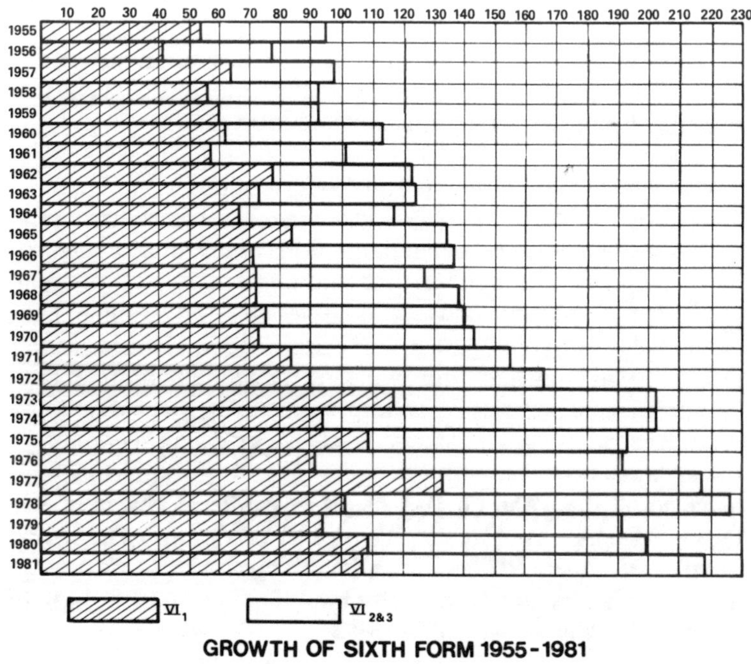

GROWTH OF SIXTH FORM 1955-1981

training after leaving school. It seemed that this was becoming generally recognised, for by 1982 the Sixth Form numbered 19.4 per cent of the whole school. In 1913 in its earlier years it was 8 per cent, in 1923 in the years of the junior school expansion it had dropped to 4.3 per cent, by 1932 it had again climbed to 7.9 per cent. The end of the Second World War in 1949 saw it at 7 per cent, but by 1956 its value had become recognised, and it formed 13.4 per cent, and thereafter it has grown steadily reaching 15 per cent in 1967.

As far as buildings are concerned, 1981 saw the new Home Economics room put into use, while the new Sports Hall is nearing completion. Across Cardington Road, the Coach House of Howard House has been converted into a new Music block, ultimately for the Preparatory Department in 1982. The Boarding House closed in the summer of 1981, and Howard House is being adapted for the enlarged Preparatory Department. This is one of the results of Independence, for the Preparatory Department has been built up in order to ensure a sufficient number of pupils in the first year of the main school. While the seven-year-olds form one class in Prep. I, Prep. II consists of two classes of eight-year-olds, and Preps. III and IV have three such classes each, which, with an extra intake at eleven, it is hoped will give four first forms for the future.

Technological developments and modern trends

Though there has been no drastic change, general technological advances have been reflected in methods of teaching and learning, as well as in the increase in the numbers of girls interested in the 'Science' subjects. In Modern Languages, for example, Language Laboratory equipment was purchased in 1974 for senior girls to use in language study, working individually from tapes at comprehension exercises, or improving their own accents by recording themselves. 'Cookery' has become 'Home Economics' – the syllabus now demands the wider and more technical knowledge implied by the change of title – while Needlework has become 'Fashion and Fabrics' at Ordinary Level, and 'Fashion and Textiles' at Advanced Level, both demanding a deeper knowledge of the chemistry involved in the manufacture and finishing of synthetic, as well as natural fabrics.

Bible Knowledge, for many years a popular academic subject, has now become Religious Studies. The need in the world of today for a deeper knowledge and understanding of other religions is recognised, while maintaining its academic standards and a steady stream of girls read Theology at university.

Freed from the disadvantages of being a compulsory subject at Ordinary Level for University entrance, a new impetus has been given to the more gradual modernisation of approach to learning Latin. New and lively texts suitable for use from the start give practice in reading which is essential for the enjoyment of Latin authors, while its subject matter – life in Roman times – provides valuable background information. Expeditions to plays and places of interest, such as Bath, have been made, some in conjunction with B.M.S. and B.H.S., and it is hoped to repeat 1981's visit to Rome again this year (1982).

Economics is now offered as an Advanced Level option, and in 1979/80 nineteen Sixth Form girls took part in 'Young Enterprise Companies, Bedford Area' organised by the British Institute of Management. In all, 150 students from twelve schools in the Bedford area were formed into five Companies. Each Company operated for two hours on one evening per week for seven to eight months. Volunteer Advisers (people experienced in finance, accountancy, marketing, personnel management, etc), gave up their spare time to guide the students in the formation of the Companies and were available in an advisory capacity throughout the programme. The aim was to enable the students to learn at first hand how business works – at all levels – from shop floor to management.

In September 1981 the school acquired its first micro-computers. Sixteen members of staff took part in courses on the use of micro-computers in education held in school during the holidays in 1981, and in September, second year girls found that the use of the computer was included in their Mathematics course. It is hoped to arrange times in which members of staff and senior girls will be able to further their studies so that in future all girls will be familiar with the general use and uses of a computer before they leave school.

There has, too, been an increase in most subjects of the amount of work done outside school hours. The field courses undertaken by Biology and Geography groups have already been mentioned, but the Alternative Ordinary Level Human Biology and the Advanced Level Home Economics courses now have part of the syllabus devoted to community studies, involving an interesting programme of lectures and visits. Other subjects have profited from inter-school discussions, while from 1978 sixth form girls studying Advanced Level History have attended the Renaissance Society lectures at University College, London, and also the National Portrait Gallery lectures for sixth formers, and from 1980 an annual History weekend has been arranged for First Form girls at Netherswell.

Music

Under Miss Grigg's able direction, and fired by her enthusiasm, musical activities continued to flourish. The Senior Choir was one of the choirs singing in the television programme *Songs of Praise*.

Highlights were undoubtedly the twenty-fifth Vellore Concert at the Royal Albert Hall when one hundred girls from Dame Alice combined with five hundred other singers from Bedfordshire choirs to perform *Belshazzar's Feast* by Sir William Walton. On another occasion the school took part in a performance of the *Messiah* when the proceeds were sent to the British National Committee for the Prevention of Blindness, and in 1981 they sang in Beethoven's *Ninth Symphony*. They have also sung at various functions in Bedford – a Civic Service to mark the opening of the new session of the Crown Court, the Annual Service for the Red Cross Society and at the Civic Carol Service in which they were joined by the Orchestra, as well as at school concerts and carol services.

There have also been many successes in the Bedfordshire Music Festival, including both individual instrumentalists, the Preparatory Choir, the Middle School Choir and the Madrigal Group.

Over the last ten years, under Miss Grigg's baton, the Upper School have given much pleasure by their lively and exciting performances of *Die Fledermaus*, *La Belle Hélène* and *The Merry Widow*.

Drama

With the appointment of a Drama Specialist, Mrs Roe, in 1976, drama work developed too. From 1977, drama lessons began to be part of the curriculum and by 1980 every girl from Prep. II to Form IV had a curriculum drama lesson. Workshops, which replaced the drama clubs, enabled the girls to enjoy an integrated programme of dramatic experience. The school plays: *The Caucasian Chalk Circle*, 1973, *Pygmalion*, 1975, *The Lark*, 1976, *Ring Round the Moon*, 1977, *The Miracle Worker*, 1978, *Hamlet*, 1980 and *Lark Rise*, 1981, became the culmination of work done throughout the year by a large number of girls.

Extracts from the Drama Report in *Uisage* 1978 give further details:

'Drama lessons in school have given girls the opportunity to develop their skills in acting and communication. All groups follow a basic course in improvisation. . . . This year we have covered many aspects of drama . . . some of these being: mime, character interpretation, understanding relationships with others, story-telling, acting in social situations, dance drama, work with masks, and shape and pacing in a play. . . . In the Fifth and Sixth forms these studies continue and time is also given to some scripted drama. Some groups have learnt the basic techniques of stage make-up.

'We entered nine improvisation groups in the Speech and Drama section of the Bedfordshire Music Festival and several girls entered individual classes. A variety of items has been presented at school concerts. . . .

'In November, in conjunction with the English Department at Bedford Modern School, some Fifth year girls and boys took part in a series of rehearsal play readings of selected scenes from *Macbeth*, this year's O-level play. These performances were followed by discussion groups of Fifth year students from both schools, led by the English staff.

'At present our major drama activity is in progress . . . we are very grateful for the help and support we are receiving from other departments in the school. We have been most fortunate to have our lighting system modernised. This has been made possible by the generosity of the P.T.A. This means that girls taking Physics and having a particular interest in lighting will be able to design and work lights for the production. . . . The P.T.A. have also helped us by purchasing a set of rostra for use in productions and drama lessons.'

Community concern

Concern for the community at large has always been part of the school tradition. The early connection with Dr Barnardo's Homes, the regular Guild of Help collections, the annual display of Guild garments made by the girls for those in need, have already been mentioned. The girls themselves became more directly involved in community work with the holding of the Christmas Tree Party, first recorded in 1927 when about 50 children were entertained with games by school and form captains, given tea, and after a visit from Santa Claus, sent home with a present. This has become an annual event – accounts indicate that though the entertainments may have become more sophisticated – 'VI$_1$ provided great delight with their pantomime *Cinderella* in 1969' – the enjoyment has remained constant. In 1929 'our little guests were, with difficulty, induced to turn their attention to such mundane things as hats and coats, and finally, each clasping a bag of sweets and an orange, besides the fascinating brown parcel, they departed in a happy mood,' while 40 years later the 'members of VI$_2$ seemed to enjoy the games as much as the guests – it was quite a sight to see them running round the hall with the children.' Father Christmas, too, has remained 'the climax of the afternoon.'

Contact has been maintained in this more personal way with the various Children's Homes in the locality, forms making presents, or preparing stockings for each child individually at Christmas, while it has also been established with Old People's Homes throughout the town, and of course the Harpur Trust almshouses. In addition to work done by individual members, the Old Girls' Association has held an annual party for the Blind, at which members of the Sixth Form have assisted.

This willingness to serve has now been organised into 'Youth Action' – formerly Bedford Schools' Community Service Council. A full-time Community Service Volunteer and a central committee copes with the organisation required, while a grant from the Harpur Trust helps with the purchase of necessary equipment. Volunteers from senior pupils of the Harpur Trust Schools and those of Bedford's Upper Schools who later joined the scheme, have been very active in all kinds of community service.

The 1972 *Uisage* reports: 'Youth Action has continued to flourish at this school. Our range of activities has broadened. . . . In addition to the usual visiting, decorating and hairdressing activities we managed to entertain the residents of Harpur House on several occasions. Our activities at the school-phobic club and the B.I.F.A. play-groups have continued and our help in the canteen at Bromham Hospital on Sunday afternoons during the Summer term and the vacation of 1971 was also successful. A few of our older members have once again taken part in the flag-selling operations for the British Red Cross Society.' A major event of the following year was 'the Christmas Service at Trinity Church, organised for the elderly citizens of the town. Despite the enormous task of finding transport for everybody, it was eventually achieved and the service gave pleasure to all involved. In September 1974 Youth Action appointed a permanent organising secretary. . . . Her hard work and determination have meant greater activity and this year project work has become more varied. Some volunteers helped to decorate the dining room in the Guild House, Harpur Street. . . .' Activities and efforts have been maintained and Youth Action is still continuing to serve.

The 1980 Charities' Report reads thus: 'Along with the Harvest Festival and Christmas charities, girls raised £820 for the Oxfam Blue Peter Appeal for Cambodia and about £1,000 for Cancer Research. . . . Individual girls also raised money for the following charities: R.N.I.B., the British Heart Foundation, Sue Ryder Foundation, St John's, Moggerhanger, the Bedfordshire and Huntingdonshire Naturalists' Trust, Save the Children Fund, Jimmy Savile's Appeal for Stoke Mandeville Hospital and the East African Emergency Appeal.' The Preparatory Department had their own special charity – the harness and fees for training a guide dog.

This tradition of community service has been maintained beyond the boundaries of school. In its early years several girls spent a year in Voluntary Service Overseas, but since 1971 V.S.O. has accepted trained volunteers (e.g. qualified doctors, nurses, teachers, etc) rather than school leavers. Several leavers, too, have spent a year as Community Service Volunteers before entering university or continuing further training for the career of their choice, while through the years many Old Girls have continued to serve as individuals, or in the many organisations which care for those in need.

Physical Education

In Bromham Road

'Games did not play an important part when the school was very young; indeed they were not on the timetable at all. The juniors played captain, stag and other games at break, but there was nothing for the seniors. Some of us learnt to play cricket well in the holidays and we thought it would be nice to continue the game at school as long as the fine weather lasted. We possessed a bat – of sorts – and a ball, while the trees – not so tall nor as portly as they are now – would provide excellent wickets, so why not? We did! For about a week, possibly less, we played before afternoon school and all was well. Then the 'Powers that Were' happened to arrive extra early, and, unfortunately, so had many schoolboy spectators along the railings. The result of this 'most unlady-like conduct' was to have boards fixed in front of our part of the playground and henceforth we played whatever games we had the heart for in convent-like seclusion.

'There was one severe winter when the school was very young, and then, as now, sliding presented a great attraction to schoolgirls. Someone began a long slide just outside the school and each girl or passing boy added to it until it extended almost to the middle gates. Of course, it was not exactly the right place in which to indulge in such a pastime, but we enjoyed it until those in authority arrived. What was thought of "such disgraceful conduct", we heard after prayers!

'As for gymnastics, they did not exist either. Certainly the word DRILL was on the timetable nearly every day, but it was not what you girls understand by it nowadays. We merely stood in lines between the desks and did a few arm and leg exercises. With hands on hips we endeavoured to bend our knees, but more often bruised our elbows against the desks on either side, or else overbalanced. . . .

'In 1887, after the children had gone home on Friday afternoons, the staff, with the Headmistress, gathered in the gymnasium or in an empty classroom and had lessons in Swedish

Drill from a very young Miss Stansfeld; these lessons we duly passed to the children later on.

'What a wonderful innovation was the gym. class when Miss Stansfeld arrived on the scene with the Swedish Drill . . . we did not really own her, but shared her with the High School. We looked forward to gym. days.

'The Commercial Baths were a great joy in summer, and many free afternoons, as well as Saturdays, were spent there.'

In St. Paul's Square

'As soon as it was possible, gymnastics were placed under the supervision of Miss Stansfeld, who undertook to provide instructors from her own staff. The connection of the school with the Physical Training College has been of incalculable value to the girls, and like so many schools of varying types in the town, the Girls' Modern School owes an immense debt of gratitude to Miss Stansfeld and her staff for their most generous help in every possible way.

'Girls were allowed Thursday as a half to go to the baths if they had not more than 2 returned lessons in the Upper or 3 in the Lower School this did not answer well the lessons for the next day being badly prepared for younger children.' – (from Miss Dolby's 'Log')

'At first the only provision for games was an asphalt tennis court in the school playground. This was in constant use and tennis tournaments were played in the Summer term. Hockey soon began . . . The school's first games of hockey . . . took place in the playground . . . which was spacious and sloped gently down towards the river. The older girls and mistresses were hampered by long skirts and voluminous petticoats underneath, and the ball persisted in rolling down the slope towards the river, unless, for a change, it hid itself among the ivy and wisteria that covered a red brick wall. Hockey under such conditions was a hot and somewhat exhausting game. We had no permanent field. One was rented wherever available each winter, and the girls played with much spirit. Matches with other schools and clubs were arranged, and finally the field in Chaucer Road was taken in 1910. A pavilion was put up later. . . .

'There was a small wooden hut in which to keep our outdoor

clothes, but we played in our gymslips and blouses, only changing from shoes to boots for hockey, and to plimsolls when playing rounders. There was no water supply for drinking or washing. Girls who did not play hockey played netball in the school playground.

'Netball was introduced in 1903 and has always been popular. Rounders was played with much enthusiasm for some years and matches with other schools were a great feature of the summer term. A cricket club was formed in 1902, and cricket was played from time to time with varying success.

'. . . the annual (from July 1907) swimming races in the Commercial baths – a great thrill to form a long procession trailing to and fro; the whole school marched out from St. Paul's Square in one long line – do you remember the muddy river water?'

While the annual swimming races appear to have been abandoned, two of the annual events – the Gym. Competition, and Sports' Day – continued after the school moved to Cardington Road. Excerpts give an idea of some of the changes that took place over the years.

Gymastic Competition 1907–1952

'May 22 & 29: Class Gymnastic Competition by Miss Stansfeld, Shield won by III Lower A.' (Held annually from 1907 – two shields Upper and Lower School from 1908.)

'The work of the Upper School this year (1934) . . . was not quite so accurate as usual, but one can perhaps set against the loss in accuracy the greatly improved carriage and posture of the girls – nearly every girl seems to know the secret of a good posture, and how to correct a bad one. . . . In the Middle School IV Lower A was the best form, it was much the most vigorous, its members held themselves well, and their climbing and balance-walking was good.

'The work in the Junior School was a very great pleasure to see. The forms were very earnest and hardworking, and so intent on the business in hand that this work was very controlled for such little people. They stopped exactly when they were told, worked with very great spirit, and did very careful apparatus work. . . .

'Instead of the usual annual gymnastic competition, this year (1951) the senior school combined to give a display of dancing and gymnastics to which parents and friends were invited.

'The whole school took part in the competition this year, (1952) and by working to a strict fifteen minute timetable we were able to judge all the forms in one day. All work was done in the gymnasium and no spectators were allowed, this meant less upset to the curriculum of the school. . . .' (This appears to be the last of the annual competitions: the increased numbers in the school obviously made organisation very difficult.)

Sports Day 1909–1980

The first Sports Day, for the Third forms and Lower School was held in 1909. The Upper School had its own Sports Day in 1913 – with a note 'No brothers admitted'. Thereafter the whole School had a combined Sports Day. The Coronation Sports Programme on page 160 is fairly typical.

In 1964 Sports' Day was for the Junior School only, the Seniors holding an Athletics Session, and in 1966 Sports' Day gave way entirely to Athletics. It was, however, revived in 1980.

In Cardington Road

For the Games activities in general 26th October 1929 was a 'red-letter day': 'Miss Tonkin invited the Governors of the School to an official opening of our new field. Besides Miss Tonkin and the majority of the staff, the Governors present were: Messrs A. Scott-Cooper and H. S. Deacon of the Governors of the Harpur Trust, Mr H. W. Liddle, M.A., Mrs Liddle and Mr G. P. Allen, F.R.I.B.A. (Surveyor to the Trust), who was responsible for the layout of the field, the total cost of which was approximately £2,850. A large number of girls also came to support the School. Two hockey matches were played. . . . The white goal posts and the new flags, which Miss McVie presented to the School last term, made the pitches look very smart.' There were four new tennis courts, the grass 'grown from seed', with an extra six marked on the hockey pitches for the Summer term, and two rounders pitches. The first hard tennis courts were the gift of the Parents' Association and were opened on 2nd October 1937.

The next landmark came when the school itself moved to

THE DAME ALICE HARPUR SCHOOL, BEDFORD

CORONATION SPORTS PROGRAMME

Thursday, June 25th, 1953, 2.15 p.m.

---

1. **Flat Race** (9—11 years)
2. **Throwing** (13—15 years)
3. Steering Race ... ... III and IV Forms
4. Three-legged Race ... I and II Forms
5. Poodle and Shoe Race ... Prep. 1, 2, 3
6. **JUNIOR SCHOOL RELAY**

HOUSE HOCKEY BALL DRIBBLING

7. **Flat Race** (11—13 years)
   (15 and over)
8. **Throwing** (9 11 years)
9. Centipede Race ... ... V Forms
10. Wheelbarrow Race ... ... I Forms
11. Potato Race ... ... III and IV Forms
12. Skipping Race ... ... Prep. 1, 2, 3

HOUSE NETBALL SHOOTING COMPETITION

13. **SENIOR HOUSE RELAY**
14. **Flat Race** (13—15 years)
15. **Throwing** (11—13 years)
    (15 and over)
16. Flower Pot Race ... ... III Forms

QUEEN ELIZABETH STEEPLE CHASE

17. Grand National ... ... VI Forms
18. Sack Race ... ... II Forms
19. Coronation Ride ... ... VI Upper
20. **JUNIOR HOUSE RELAY**
21. **Flat Race** (7—9 years)
22. Nautical Race ... ... IV Forms
23. Egg and Spoon Race ... I and II Forms
24. Obstacle Race ... ... V and VI Forms
25. **Parent and Teacher Race (Fathers)**
26. **Mothers' and Daughters' Race**
27. **DEMONSTRATION OF JUMPING by the Winners**

Cardington Road: Miss Tonkin reported 'the previous arrangement with Miss Stansfeld has been dissolved by agreement. I have appointed a full-time mistress for Physical Training so that each class will be able to have two forty-minute periods in place of two twenty-minute periods, as well as the usual games period and voluntary games.' When Miss De La Mare left in 1944 she was succeeded by two full-time P.E. mistresses, Miss Burnell-Carter, and Miss Neel.

Swimming

Swimming continued to flourish: 'the new baths at the Boys' Modern School field' had been opened during the Autumn term of 1935 and thereafter were used by the girls regularly on one or two afternoons a week for the next fifteen years. 'In spite of only two hours' coaching time in the baths each week, 160 girls, divided into fifteen classes, were able to be coached regularly . . . many non-swimmers were able to swim by the end of term,' but difficulties of time and numbers were somewhat daunting, and there seemed to be a decline in enthusiasm as the 'fifties proceeded. In 1957 among the gifts to commemorate the 75th birthday, three forms gave a 'contribution to start a swimming pool fund'. Thereafter many school efforts were devoted to the increase of this fund until it ceased to exist, in 1970. . . . 'In the year after the opening of the Swimming Pool, 52 girls have taken the A.S.A. Personal Survival Awards, and 30 girls have gained the Bronze Medallion of the Royal Life Saving Society.'

General Expansion and Development

For P.E. in general, the years following the opening of the Swimming Pool have been years of rapid expansion and development. By 1970 compulsory rounders had disappeared, while Athletics developed from the mid 1950s to earn a section in the Games report of *Uisage* 1972. 'In May 1971 we entered the Bedford and District Schools' Championships for the first time.' In the following year three teams entered: 'five girls gained first places and thus represented Bedford at the County Finals. . . .'

In the same year the team of swimmers who represented the school in the Secondary Schools' Swimming Gala won the Robinson Cup, while 'Olympic gymnastic clubs have now become firmly established as part of the extra-curricular activities.'

1975/76 was a year of success:

'Nine girls gained places in either the 1st or 2nd Junior County Hockey teams and one girl was chosen for the second year running to play in the Midland Junior County 2nd XI.

'Seven girls were selected for the County Netball teams and five others were co-opted during the season.

'Three girls played Junior County Tennis. One girl was in the Eastern Region tournament team which was placed first.

'In the Bedfordshire Schools' Tournaments the 1st and Under 16 yrs. Hockey teams were both placed first. The 1st and Under 13 yrs. Netball teams were both placed first, and the Intermediate and Junior Tennis couples were placed first in their sections.

'In the Bedford and District Schools' Swimming Gala our senior team tied with the High School team in first place (to share the Robinson Bowl).

'Members of the Life Saving Clubs have worked enthusiastically. Six girls worked for their Teacher's Certificate by preparing groups of four or more candidates for the Bronze Medallion and a total of 55 other awards have been gained.

'At the Bedford and District Athletics meeting our intermediate team won the cup for the sixth year running and both the Senior and Junior teams were placed second. Nine girls went on to represent Bedford and District at the County finals and one girl qualified in the hurdles and relay events for the A.A.A.'s Schools' Championships for the third year running.

'Gymnastics clubs for all age groups continue to be very popular. Many more girls have gained B.A.G.A. awards and some have reached a very high standard. The work shown at the gymnastic display in March was very good. Some girls have extra coaching at other clubs in the town. One girl was first in her age group in the Bedfordshire Championships. She gained second place in the Eastern Region and went on to represent the East in the National Championships.'

A Cricket Club was once again revived in 1973 (there had been a dinner-hour club for a short time in the early fifties), three of its members visiting Lord's cricket ground and demonstrating the new tests in front of the pavilion, thus making history – previously girls had never been allowed to play cricket at Lord's. In 1979/80 'matches were played against a number of schools including Sandy Upper School and Redbourne School, Ampthill,' while 'the House system enabled a greater number of the younger players to gain experience under match conditions'.

1981 has seen extensions to the hard tennis courts so that they can be used as netball courts now that the Sports Hall covers the old, while two netball/tennis courts have been provided in the grounds of Howard House.

The present P.E. activities contrast with the simplicity of the 'old' hockey, netball, rounders, tennis, swimming, gym and dance.

While the juniors (preps. and forms I–III) have set activities, the seniors (IV form upwards) have a choice which includes swimming, games, keep-fit, country dancing, volley-ball, badminton, table-tennis, squash, golf and trampolining. Extra-curricular clubs include trampolining, gymnastics, badminton, table-tennis, swimming, with the winter hockey and netball giving way to cricket, athletics, tennis, and rounders in the summer.

The new Sports Hall will give additional facilities for existing indoor sports to which it is hoped to add basketball, while dark nights and wet weather can be ignored.

The P.E. Department has also taken parties of girls on courses during the holidays – ski-ing for a week at Easter, and in the summer a one-week sailing course on board the frigate *Foudroyant* at Portsmouth, and a week's Adventure Holiday in Devon, which included surfing, diving and snorkelling, archery, golf, riding and rifle-shooting.

Boarders and the Boarding Houses

'The boarding house was a vital part of the school. It began in 1895, in a house in Chaucer Road, with one solitary boarder; next term there were two, and by degrees the numbers increased until a larger house was needed. Then we migrated, in 1902, to 8 Lansdowne Road, where we remained until 1918. For the last part of this time a second house in Lansdowne Road was taken. Miss Buckley and Miss Fish (Mrs Dale) lived here and took charge of about six girls, who slept here but spent the day at No. 8, which was the best plan it was possible to make during the war years. As soon as circumstances allowed, a larger house in Shakespeare Road was taken and enlarged, and we moved into it at Easter 1918. It was a sunny, roomy house and accommodated about twenty-nine girls. Also it was close to the school field, a great advantage. The girls all came back that Summer term full of excitement to the new house and settled down there very happily.' – Miss Dolby in *Uisage* 1932.

One of the boarders of these years was Kathleen Easmon, whose death was reported in the Old Girls' Leaflet of 1925. 'One of the most cultured women that West Africa has yet given to the world passed away at the early age of 32 at Charing Cross Hospital. This was Mrs K. Simango, A.R.C.A., daughter of Dr Easmon, late Principal M.O. of Sierra Leone, one of the first coloured medical men to get his degree in London. As Miss Kathleen Easmon she came to England to complete her education at the Girls' Modern School, Bedford. . . . and later she studied art at South Kensington. When quite a girl she wrote the lyrics for the late Coleridge-Taylor's *My Lady Moon* cycle of songs. She met her husband, Mr Mamba Simango, an East African who had taken his B.Sc. and Teacher's Diploma at Columbia University, N.Y., when she travelled in America, raising funds to provide for the establishment in W. Africa of a modern demonstration school for girls. It was their intention to start a similar school for boys and girls under the American Board of Missions in Portuguese E. Africa.'

'My mother was so impressed with the finesse and other attributes of the late Kathleen Easmon (our cousin) when she returned to West Africa that she decided her children would also go to Bedford for schooling.

'In 1927, my father brought me to England from Freetown, Sierra Leone, for schooling. My grandfather and I visited other schools, but Bedford Modern School for Girls was decided upon. There was no boarding house as such, but Miss Winifred Crump, a teacher at the school, who lived at 45 Chaucer Road, looked after girls whose parents were either abroad or lived some distance from Bedford. There were only 12 of us, including myself, when I came to school. Those who did not go home for half-term used to club together and have midnight feasts, which were enjoyable, provided we were not caught. . . .

'My sister (Frances) and brother (B.M.S.) joined me, followed by my cousin Sophie Wright. . . . On leaving school, I took up Secretarial Training in London, my brother did Dentistry in Edinburgh, and my cousin did Medicine. Both my sister and I live in Freetown, where she is still practising (Frances became a barrister and is mentioned earlier) and I am still in harness as a secretary. My son, Francis, attended B.M.S. 1967–75.' (Eva Wright, 1979.)

Miss Crump retired from teaching in 1935, but kept the charge of the boarders until March 1944. She had then been in charge for nearly twenty years. It was not until 1950 that Margaret House, Bushmead Avenue was opened as a boarding house beginning with twelve girls. In the second term there were 22, 'including one Persian, one Armenian and one African,' increasing to thirty-four in 1952 and reaching its full complement of thirty-six in the following year. In addition, between thirty and forty day girls had dinner there, as the dining facilities at school were so limited.

From 1955 to 1970 the boarders numbered 36 to 40: the house was barely adequate for the larger number – there was no quiet room for reading, nor a waiting room for visitors and parents, and the garden was too small for most outdoor activities. The acquisition of Howard House by the Governors in 1969 was therefore most welcome, and the number of boarders was increased to 49.

With the increased facilities, the boarders were able to develop their own activities: in 1972–73 a group of girls began working for the Bronze Award of the Duke of Edinburgh Award Scheme, with lectures on First Aid, the Police Service, and Cosmetics. 'Some senior girls go to a Judo club, and some junior girls attend Guides. This term, arrangements have been made for fortnightly meetings on a Sunday evening, sometimes at Howard House, and sometimes at Talbot House, Bedford School, for discussion of religious matters and for social activities.'

With the coming of Independence the question of boarding was carefully considered and after much discussion it was decided to phase out boarding. The final closure of Howard

House as a boarding house came in July 1981, instead of 1983, alternative arrangements being made for the accommodation of existing boarders. It will re-open in the Centenary year for the Preparatory Department.

Careers

What of the future? This is a question often asked concerning independent schools today, but it is far more relevant when asked concerning the education given in a school, than of the school itself. The whole purpose of founding schools for girls was to educate them to play their full part in the community. The emancipation of women opened many doors, and the continuing movement towards complete equality has given girls wider opportunities and greater freedom of choice than ever before. They must therefore be educated to use these opportunities and to make their choice wisely.

This was recognised by Sir Charles Cheers Wakefield, Lord Mayor of London 1915–16, in his book, *On Leaving School and the Choice of a Career*, first published in 1927. As part of a series of Lenten addresses on various aspects of education given in St. Martin's, Ludgate, he had been asked to take 'Education and Commerce' as his subject. The book was a consequence of this, for as he says in the foreword, 'The more I pondered on the difficult problems of the choice of a career, as it presents itself to young men and women today, the more vital seemed to me its relation to the problems of education . . . education and their preparation for the work of the world is probably our most important duty in life.' By the time this book was acquired for the school library about 1937, it had reached its 21st edition. Sir Charles' concern, reflecting that of the business and commercial interests of the City, was obviously widely shared.

Though many schools recognised the importance of this vocational guidance, and some had a member of staff responsible for helping school leavers find employment, national recognition of the problem was extremely slow in developing. Not until 1959 did the Ministry of Education introduce its short training courses for Careers teachers, and not until ten years later was the National Association of Careers Teachers founded – two members of the Dame Alice Harpur School staff were present at its inaugural conference. The Old Girls' Association from the first showed a keen interest in careers for women, addresses on different aspects of the subject being given at the first three general meetings.

The earliest recorded general careers guidance at school, however, comes from the years when it was still in St. Paul's Square. In the fourth issue of *Uisage*, March 1930, is a report entitled 'Careers for Girls – I – The Civil Service'. This lecture was one of two given by a parent to the Parents' Association at a meeting to which older girls were invited: the second was on 'The Local Government Service', a summary of which was printed in the sixth issue. It is interesting today to note that in 1930 'all girls have to resign on marriage' in the Civil Service, and that salaries range from about £230 to £390 in the Administrative Posts which require nomination, to '8s to 35s (a week)' for 'telephonists in the "Provinces".' In the Local Government Service 'conditions of service are improving rapidly. About forty-four hours are worked weekly, with occasional overtime (unpaid), and sickness is covered by salary, and in addition to payments from the National Health Insurance, superannuation is payable in most of the large Authorities. (Not in Beds. at present.) Good holidays are given in addition to Bank Holidays.'

In the same issue as the account of the Local Government Service is a report of Miss Wright's 'interesting lecture on Nursing' which concludes, 'Girls taking up nursing will learn a profession with practically no cost to their parents, and will rise with girls of their own social standing; but they should choose their training school carefully and send to the matron for particulars and forms to fill up.'

Librarianship was dealt with in the July 1931 *Uisage*, opening 'A great development of library activity is probable in the future.' Details of qualifications and training are given including 'A foreign language is essential *besides* Greek or Latin. . . . Vacancies are few and intending students should obtain practical experience in a local library first.' The next number of *Uisage* dealt with 'The Teaching Profession'.

The same careers were dealt with, though perhaps more fully, in a new series of talks arranged by the Parents' Association in 1934. Teaching, for instance, is divided into Elementary and

Secondary School Teaching, with additional mention of specialised branches, such as Art, Domestic Science, Physical Training and Kindergarten. A new career is outlined – that of Poultry Husbandry with its need for 'a good general education' followed by training at a Farm Institute leading to a National Diploma, or at an Agricultural College. Two years later 'Miss Tacon-Gilbert gave much more interesting information, illustrated by lantern slides, on outdoor careers for girls.' This included market-gardening, fruit culture, flower growing, dairy work, as well as poultry farming, noting 'When embarking on farming of any sort, great attention should be paid to the choice of district. Breeding is interesting work, but requires skill and study as well as capital. Pigs are at present the most profitable animals to breed; also foxes, musquash and rabbits for their furs.' Riding School instructors, Kennel Assistants and Canine Nurses – 'very good posts are available for girls who do the five years' course at a Veterinary College (fees £35 to £50)' – were all mentioned, the talk concluding with the mention of the Physical Training diploma which qualified for work in schools and clubs, and also for masseuses. There appears to be no mention of the Police Force though Mary Wilkinson had joined the Women's Auxiliary Service in 1931.

By this date Doreen Henry had already qualified as a masseuse at Anstey Physical Training College, while the same number of *Uisage*, July 1934, lists three girls qualified as Art mistresses, the gaining of a London B.A. degree by another, a success in a Civil Service examination, a qualified Norland nurse and concludes with an extract from 'The East African Standard' entitled 'Miss Mary Leonard's Success – First Woman Accountant and Auditor in Kenya.' The report congratulated her on being the pioneer woman accountant and auditor in East Africa, and also mentioned that she was well-known throughout Kenya as a golfer, having won the Ladies' Championship in 1932. Mary left school in 1929.

One Old Girl who made a name for herself in music was Dorothy Erhart, one of the first members of the Association. Little detail is given, but the 1926 Leaflet reports: 'On November 3rd an enterprising programme was given in the Mortimer Hall by a small string orchestra under the conductorship of Dorothy

Erhart. Two movements were played from a Violincello Concerto by Porpora which she had transcribed from the MS in the British Museum.' The following year three concerts were given by The Erhart String Chamber Orchestra in the Mortimer Hall, and the leaflet also mentioned the Choral Society she ran at Withyham, Sussex. In 1937 she was accompanying and coaching singers at the Webber-Douglas School of Music, and conducting two amateur orchestras and a choir. The Erhart String Chamber Orchestra was giving a concert on 27th March – she herself was playing the solo harpsichord in Bach's Concerto in F Minor. She was also Music Adviser to the Joint Committee for Music and Drama in Villages, travelling all over the country, visiting and advising local groups. During the Second World War 'she did a great deal for the C.E.M.A., playing and conducting at village concerts, Land Army Hostels, and so on: she also adjudicated at many Music Festivals and is now connected with the Arts Council.' – (1946 Leaflet.)

From the early days, then, a wide variety of careers was followed by Old Girls, not only in the British Isles, but in many countries throughout the world. It was obvious that a great deal of interest was taken by Miss Dolby, and Miss Tonkin, and their teaching staff, in the careers of their girls, and the smaller numbers in the school in those years made individual interest and personal advice relatively easy. The disruptions of the war years, both within and without the school, together with the rapid increase in numbers, meant that a more organised approach to careers was needed. In 1949, the Inspectors reported that the careers taken up by school leavers had been somewhat disappointing: of the 337 who had left during the past three years 92 had gone into clerical work, and only 35 to places of further education, including the 15 who entered universities.

It was after this that Miss Pengilly added the work of Careers Mistress to the teaching of Mathematics, using as her 'base' the medical room in Dame Alice House, storing pamphlets and prospectuses in the large walk-in cupboard there. It was this room, when not in use as a medical room, that Miss W. Dickson inherited on her appointment as Careers Mistress in 1959. Many a girl or member of staff, on reaching the room, has remarked, rather breathlessly, 'You have to be fit to come up all these stairs!' Medicals were soon transferred to a more convenient place, and the medical room became known as the Careers room. Because of its increasing volume the literature was re-catalogued and the theory that the best counselling could only be given if the client came voluntarily to seek it was discarded in favour of the practice of group discussion with three or four girls. If the discussion was slow to start, disappearance of staff into the cupboard in search of a pamphlet seemed to unlock the tongues!

One result of these discussions was the distribution of literature to individual students, and with the opening of the Douglas Gordon Building the old sixth form studio became the Careers Display Centre. Shelves and wall racks with displays of literature replaced the murals, and work tops and chairs made it a place where girls could come and browse whenever they had the opportunity. A second display area was later set up in the entrance hall of the Douglas Gordon Building. About the same time the old 'property cupboard' was absorbed into the Careers area, to be used as an extra interview room and office.

During the 1960s and early 1970s the pattern of careers lessons gradually developed. The problem was finding time to insert extra lessons into the curriculum. With an eight period day and the abandonment of British Standard Time it was too dark to have games lessons or practices in the last period of afternoon school, so careers talks by outside speakers, and lessons of a general nature were introduced for the fifth forms. Miss Durham, of the History Department, became involved in Careers work at this stage, and together she and Miss Dickson experimented with various activities – one of the more successful being the mock interview. When ordinary Summer Time was resumed, Careers lessons had become established on a regular weekly basis for the fifth forms.

About this time, some sixth-formers were beginning to regret their choice of subjects for O-level, made on entering the fourth form. They found that by opting out of subjects, particularly the sciences, they were not qualified for courses they wished to follow on leaving school. Lunch hour discussions with individual third-formers (13+) were introduced, and went a little way towards solving the problem. With the re-organisation for the

13+ entry an arrangement was made whereby the French department had an extra lesson in the Autumn term, and for the Spring and Summer terms a programme of Careers lessons became part of the Third-year curriculum.

It now became obvious that a link – lessons for the fourth year – was necessary and after some experiment these have been arranged in private study time as each fourth-former has at least one private study period on her timetable. Groups of varying sizes have been formed and a series of ten lessons runs from the Spring term into the Summer term. Lessons in the Lower Sixth were also established, once again a ten-week course during the Autumn and Spring terms.

The pioneering work for all these courses was done by Miss Dickson and Miss Durham. Gradually other members of staff became involved, and by planned in-service training, staff new to the Careers team learned by going to the lessons of established Careers staff for a complete session. This training was supported by several after-school sessions at which members of the Local Careers Service initiated topics and led discussions on a variety of fundamental ideas.

The emergence of the present structure was gradual, over a period of ten years or so, and was complete earlier than in many schools. Each pupil in the school from the age of 13+ has a careers tutor with whom she and her parents can discuss any aspect of subject or career choice. That this has been possible is a tribute to Miss Lawson Brown, who recognised the value of having a Careers Mistress with part-time teaching commitments, rather than adding all the Careers work to an assistant mistress with an already full subject teaching timetable. Its present development, with time to interview all members of the fifth and sixth forms at least once each year, as well as third and fourth form students, is an indication of the value placed on this aspect of education by Miss Morse.

At present the school has a Head of Careers Education, an Assistant Careers Mistress and five other members of staff who work in the various year groups. All the Careers tutors are teaching members of staff and belong to a variety of subject disciplines – Physics, History, English, Chemistry, Mathematics and Needlework.

The complete course offered in the three years from Form III upwards introduces the need for thinking ahead, formulating and discussing ideas with the members of staff concerned, before making decisions on the choice of subjects.

Vocational Choice by Peter March and Michael Smith forms the basis for fourth year discussion, while fifth-formers go on to the discussion of personal qualities, the world of work, applying and being interviewed, confidential reports, the Connolly Interest Questionnaire and the 'mighty micro'. In the Lower Sixth there is further discussion on the content of confidential reports, while types of further education, conditions of work, living away from home, present trends in work, such as the micro-chip revolution are some of the other subjects considered. At this stage, too, qualified parents have given assistance with mock interviews which help to prepare the girls for the challenge of the 'real thing'.

Careers Conventions, as organised at first by the Local Careers Service for fifth-formers from all Bedford's schools, became so unwieldy that they were discontinued in favour of Sixth Form evenings such as those held in 1978 at Bedford Modern School on Careers in Business and Administration, and at Pilgrim School on Scientific and Technical Careers.

To cater for the fifth form in The Dame Alice Harpur School, 'mini' Careers Conventions are held annually for girls and parents. Along with this, Easter Vacation Courses such as those in Radiography and Journalism in 1973, are organised annually by the Careers Service and both Fifth and Sixth formers derive great benefit from them. Thus, apart from work in school, advantage is taken of other opportunities offered to help girls both in choosing a career, and embarking on the career of their choice.

The careers entered by students who left The Dame Alice Harpur School during the last ten years are so varied that it is difficult to believe the restrictions that existed for girls leaving school fifty or more years ago, when many professions were virtually closed to women, while resignation upon marriage was the rule in both the teaching profession and the Civil Service. 'Equal pay for equal work' was then little more than an idealist's dream.

The analyses of destinations of school leavers (see page 173) indicate the initial stages, while information from letters sent to

DESTINATION OF SCHOOL LEAVERS

	July: 1975	*1976*	*1977*	*1978*	*1979*	*1980*	*1981*
Sixth form leavers (post A-level) ..	105	81	96	79	118	94	78
(first year)	4	7	7	3	4	5	8
Fifth form leavers	28	33	56	78	52	52	48
	137	121	159	160	174	151	134

	1975	1976	1977	1978	1979	1980	1981
(a) To full-time Further Education:							
(i) Universities.....................	35	41	36	34	49	35	41
(ii) Degree courses other than B.Ed., and (i)	10	9	9	6	18	8	10
(iii) B.Ed, courses (inc. Teacher Training 1975–77)........................	23	8	4	2	5	4	3
(iv) Art courses	—	1	3	1	2	1	—
(v) Radiography...................	3	—	—	—	1	1	1
(vi) Occupational Therapy....	—	1	1	1	1	1	1
(vii) Physiotherapy................	3	—	1	1	—	4	—
(viii) Osteopathy	—	—	—	—	—	—	1
(ix) Post A-level courses (Business, Catering, etc)..	11	8	13	9	13	6	2
(x) A-level/O-level courses at Colleges of Further Education:							
Ex-sixth forms	4	2	7	2	1	7	13
Ex-fifth forms	4	4	7	11	4	3	6
(xi) A-level/O-level courses at other schools	4	6	6	7	9	22	25
(xii) Post O-level courses (Secretarial, Business Studies, Pre-nursing, Nursery Nursing, Catering, etc)	6	14	29	37	24	14	15
(xiii) Schools of Dancing, Speech & Drama, etc	1	1	—	—	—	—	—
	104	95	116	111	127	106	118
(b) Nursing.............................	13	4	7	4	8	8	7
(c) To other posts: Local Government, Banking, Commerce, etc							
Ex-sixth form...........	10	12	20	20	21	21	5
Ex-fifth form............	10	10	16	25	18	16	4
	137	121	159	160	174	151	134

school gives some idea of the progress, and also of the achievements of a few.

One writes: 'I went to the City University to study for a degree in Ophthalmic Optics. I passed my final registration exams . . . this entitled me to have the Freedom of the Spectacle Makers' Company, one of the Livery Companies, and I have recently received the Freedom of the City of London.'

Another, having graduated in Physics from Bristol University, is now studying for an M.Sc. in Radiation Physics applied to Medicine. There are others, such as

- the winner of a one year Kennedy Scholarship to Harvard University who is an assistant producer on BBC 2's *Newsnight*;
- the member of the management development programme at Barclays Bank who is now a Loans officer;
- the young lady who is now managing a somewhat exclusive dress shop on board a liner of the Holland/America Line;
- the occupational therapist who is at present an adviser to the disabled for the Social Services of one of the London Boroughs;
- the girl who spent two years in the Police Force but left because the Equality Act meant sending women police constables out alone at night;
- the number-crunching, graph-drawing systems engineer now designing and building Sonar systems for the Navy;
- the associate member of the Institute of Personnel Managers now in the Paris Headquarters of I.C.L.;
- the temporary assistant Professor of Physics at the U.S. Naval Academy, Annapolis;
- the school teacher who is the first Lady Lieutenant in charge of the girls in both the RAF and the Army sections of her school's CCF and is involved in flying, gliding, weapon training, drill, battlecraft and camping;
- the member of the BBC Northern Symphony Orchestra;
- the psychologist who is working in the helicopter ergonomics section of the Royal Aircraft Establishment;
- the Account Planner in advertising who is studying for a Master's Degree in Management Studies;
- the clinical teacher of nurses at a London Hospital;
- the member of the Institute of Exports;

- the student who won a prize in Advanced Conservative Dentistry, and
- the one who is now Warden of a Wildfowl Trust Station, besides the professional actress, the solicitor, the local tax officer, and the cartographer.

This is but a selection: the list of interesting occupations is very long indeed, most of them needing a further period of full-time education or training after leaving school. There are very few girls today who could write as Ena Spencer did in 1928: 'I have had full control of the department since I was seventeen, and have a staff of eighteen who are all very good at their work.' She was working in the family firm – 'in our works here we make our own balloons, nets, gear and parachutes, besides other lines such as advertising kites and small balloons. When we are really busy we can turn out 100,000 balloons per week printed. . . . We can supply balloons of any sort from ½d to £3,000 each. In the summer our time is mostly taken up with Aeronautical Displays. . . . My brother and I made our first parachute descents in 1922 at Cambridge. . . .'

The situation today is far more complex, with problems of race and colour added to those of labour relations, and with all the problems posed by the new technology. Nevertheless the challenges of today are being met as has been shown: 'the development of the critical self-analysis already practised, the arousing of interest in the technology of the future, the ability to understand and use some of the new devices produced' together with an awareness of today's problems should help in looking to those of the future.

The caring professions into which many 'Dame Alice' girls go will not disappear. The development of leisure activities will demand more qualified people in a variety of fields, such as physical pursuits, entertainment, drama, and the media. Personal qualities, maturity and an ability to be flexible will enable girls to meet the challenge of the future.

In the words of the Headmistress: 'We hope that the girls who leave this school, leave it with a sense of direction. We hope that they have gained more from their time here than mere Advanced Level or Ordinary Level Certificates. We try to give them the opportunity to develop their personalities to the full –

to learn the pleasure of working hard for work's sake; to learn the pleasure of following an interest or hobby in company with others of like interest, to develop their own talents in every sphere as far as they possibly can – to enable them to live purposeful lives which are so much the richer if they are lives of service. We see no reason why these aims and ambitions should not continue to be ours in the future. . . .'

Supplement

The Houses in Cardington Road

The houses acquired have had a varied history. The 'Abbey', which was not given this name until the nineteenth century, and had no ecclesiastical connections as far as we know, except that the land may have originally belonged to the Church, probably incorporated parts of a seventeenth-century mansion built by Robert Hawes, three times Mayor of Bedford early in the century. By the end of the eighteenth century it was in the hands of Jeremy Fish Palmer, Clerk of the Peace from 1776 to 1798. He died, unmarried, in 1798 and was buried in Northill. The following description of him is from the 'Torrington diaries': 'A scud of rain hurried me into Bedford, where calling upon Mr Palmer a lawyer, I engaged myself to an early dinner. Mr P. is gouty, puddling, and knock'd up; and looks only to the main chance . . . He ordered a tench out of his stew pond, and shew'd me his garden.' At the beginning of the nineteenth century, the Abbey became the home of Jeremy's nephew Charles, M.P. for Reading, who was probably responsible for the added frontage and other alterations, since in Matthiason's description of Bedford in 1831 it is referred to as 'remarkable for its lightness and singular style'. It then passed through several hands, remaining a private residence until 1923 when a tenant, Miss Adah Mary Verey, started a Domestic Science School there which lasted until 1928, and then from 1929–1951 it was run as 'St. Mary's Abbey Hotel'.

The other three houses seem to have been linked for much of their history. The earliest reference to the 'Wing' site notes it as a 'tan-house' belonging to John Bowstred, while at the same time the rest of the land to the King's Ditch was owned by John White, the site including a house and tan vats. (It is interesting to note that Robert Hawes' grandfather Thomas, buried in St. Mary's Church, was a prosperous tanner.) The White family and the tannery continued for more than a century until 1754 when the property was sold, while the 'Wing' site, including a one-acre close of pasture land whose eastern boundary was the King's Ditch, was sold to a fell-monger who appears to have carried on his trade here until 1743. By 1757 all the property, except for one cottage by the ditch, was in the hands of a Thomas Jessop, and was then acquired by Thomas Palmer, a Bedford grocer and tallow chandler, whose heir Benjamin, sold 'Wing' site to John Wing in 1796, and left the rest to be sold by auction in 1817. John Wing, the architect, or 'builder', as he was content to call himself, demolished the existing house on the site, and built himself a new one – the present Wing House (the VI form house until 1967, Prep. House 1967–82.) When the rest of the property was put up for auction, the Dame Alice House site became a separate entity probably for the first time. It was classed as 'Lot 8' – 'all that substantial building, lately used as a schoolroom, corn chambers, coach house, stabling . . . in a capital piece of ground, well-planted with choice fruit trees . . .' and was purchased by John Wing for £370. Here he built Dame Alice House, mentioning in his will of December 1818 the house, 'new-erected' by himself. (The 'Kilpin' site was purchased by Charles Bailey, an official of the Archdeaconry of Bedford, whose wife was Benjamin Palmer's daughter.)

The Wing family remained after John's death, James Tacy Wing carrying on the family business and living in 'Wing' House until the 1840s when he bought 'Kilpin' site, moving into the house already there, and using the land at the back as a stonemason's yard. Meanwhile Frederick Howard, (later Sir Frederick) of what later became known as the 'Britannia' Iron and Steel Works, moved into 'Wing' House staying there for some years until he moved across the road, building 'Abbey Close', now 'Howard House'. Wing House was let to various tenants until it became the property of Samuel Leach Kilpin, of Kilpin and Billson – ironmongers, whose business stood at the corner of Castle Lane from the 1820s until 1927. He had previously purchased the 'Kilpin' site from J. T. Wing's widow, and he seems, judging by the complete change in the plan of the house, to have carried out extensive alterations, or perhaps entirely re-built it: thus 'Kilpin House' came into being, more or less as it stands today.

Dame Alice House was bought from the Wing family by Dr George Witt of whom 'Touchstone' of the *Bedfordshire Times* when writing of Bedford's benefactors in the mid-nineteenth century wrote: 'there were some fine doctors, men of vision as well as learning, who strove valiantly to make the town healthier and its people more receptive of ideas'. Witt was instrumental in getting tolls on the Town Bridge removed, and was concerned in the erection of the Bedford Rooms (the old Borough Library) where his museum was housed, and where many kinds of public entertainment took place. For a short time in the 1840s Witt also owned the Abbey, and was responsible for building Abbey cottage. In 1849, however, his wife's health led him to emigrate to Australia and he sold the house to Thomas Barnard, while the contents were sold by auction, Thomas Barnard buying many of the furnishings. The Barnards were a well known Bedford family, carrying on the bank founded by Thomas's father Joseph, a coal-merchant. The bank was in the block of buildings at the foot of the town bridge on the West side which was demolished when the bridge was widened:

the family also owned the house, now No. 1 St. Paul's Square, at the back of which was their original coal wharf. The Barnards retained the ownership of the house until it was sold to the Harpur Trust, but from 1860 onwards it was let to various tenants. The house appears to have been altered somewhat by 1854, the addition apparently being the room at the back with French windows into the garden, but basically the exterior was as we see it today.

Howard House, the new Prep. House, and formerly Abbey Close, was purchased by the Harpur Trust in 1969 to be used as the school boarding house. The earliest recorded dwelling on the site was a cottage belonging to Sarah Boulstred or Bowstred in 1694. The present house was built by Sir Frederick Howard to Wing's design about 1873 and Sir Frederick appears to have lived there until his death.

The Howards were a Bedford family – Frederick's grandfather John was town gaoler at the time the new prison was built *c.* 1800, and his father, also John, had been apprenticed by the Harpur Trust to an Olney ironmonger. He later set up his own shop in Bedford's High Street, and became famous for his 'improved plough' which he showed at the first Royal Agricultural Show in 1839. His sons, James and Frederick, built the Britannia Ironworks in 1859.

The original site of Abbey Close excluded much of the land and outbuildings at the back to the south-west: this belonged then to St. Mary's House. However, Sir Frederick purchased St. Mary's House in December 1875, and it became his son's home. It was this son, John Howard who inherited all the property on his father's death. He gave Abbey Close to Dr. Barnardo's for use as a children's home, the Howard Home, including in his gift most of the land and outbuildings at the back which had formerly belonged to St. Mary's House.

TEACHING STAFF 1882–1982

	Year left
1882	
Miss Cooper	1883
Miss Gillie	1885
Miss March	1885
Mrs Southgate	1885
Miss Bettison	1889
Mr Diemer	1884
Miss Abrahall	1883
Miss Lister	1894
Miss L. Buxton	1887
Mr Denyer	1886
Miss (Mlle) Truchet	1894
Miss Allen	1883
Miss Bodger (S.T.)	
Miss Boyd (S.T.)	
1883	
Miss Turner	1899
Miss Boyd (promoted to regular staff)	1884
Miss Chalker	1884
Miss Green	1884
Miss Godfrey	1887
Mrs Denyer	? 1884
Miss Bodger (S.T.)	
Miss A. Thomlinson (O.G.) (S.T.)	
1884	
Miss Crabtree	1897
Fräulein Nolden	?
Mr Blunt	?
Miss A. Thomlinson (O.G.) (Promoted to regular staff)	1899
Miss Urquhart	1885
1885	
Miss Smith	1825

(Miss Porter gives no further staff lists in her Log Book: Miss Dolby's records begin from the date of her appointment in 1894).

	Year left
1892	
Miss Clara Porter	1920
?	
Miss Brunton	1894
?	
Mlle Héron	1896
?	
Miss Denyer	1899
1895	
Miss Page	1900
Fr. Eichstedt	1896
Miss Blackwell	1896
1896	
Miss Garrett	1901
Miss Gillions (O.G.)	1934
1897	
Miss Buckley	1928
Miss Reid	1900
1899	
Miss Coltman	1929
Miss A. E. Jones	1918
Miss Shore	1900
1900	
Miss Richmond	1916
Miss Hensman	1932
Miss Stansfeld	?1912

	Year left
1901	
Miss Scruby	1902
Miss Crump	1935
1902	
Miss MacFarland	1905
also 1914 –	1932
1904	
Miss Grattan	1945
Miss E. M. Jones	1918
Miss Ames	1905
1905	
Miss Spilman	1906
Miss Whittington	1925
Miss Ryan	1906
1906	
Miss Alderson Smith	1918
Miss Martin	1936
Miss Weekes	1914
Miss Leach	1906
1907	
Miss Hadley (P.T.C.)	1918
Miss Bathurst	1909
1908	
Miss Armstrong	1909
Miss Sheldon	1909
1909	
Miss Freeth	1911–12
Miss W. Neck	1911–12
1912	
Miss Pettit	1916–17
1914	
Miss Fish (Mrs Dale)	1919
1916	
Miss Colwill (P.T.C.)	1920–21
Miss Tasker	1919

	Year left
1917	
Miss Huntington	1951
Miss Knight	1953
Miss Parker	1920
1918	
Miss Alderton	1919
Miss Blott	1920
Miss Cowling	1921
Miss Maclagan	1922
Miss Read (P.T.C.)	1921
1919	
Mrs Matkin	1942
Miss Bunney	1921
Miss Chamberlain (P.T.C.)	1922
Miss Harbon	1930
Miss Sennitt	1920
Miss Swindells	1921
Miss Webb	1921
1920	
Miss Hatton	1921
Miss Johanssen (P.T.C.)	1922
Miss Owen	1921
Miss Plummer	1924
Miss Whatley	1924
1921	
Miss Carter	1960
Miss Cranmer	1948
also part-time later	
Miss Clifford	1928
Miss Atkinson	1922
Miss Johnston (O.G.)	1925
Miss S. W. Jones	1929
Miss Warters	1923
Miss Rowlatt (P.T.C.)	1924
1922	
Miss Drury	1923
Miss Kellett	1924
Miss McMinn (P.T.C.)	1926

	Year left
1924	
Miss Faulkner	1925
Miss Howe (O.G.)	1930
as Mrs Long 1943 –	1961
Miss McVie	1929
Miss Clappen (P.T.C.)	1926
1925	
Miss Atherton	1928
1926	
Miss Dickens (O.G.)	1927
Miss Morris	1935
Miss Angus (P.T.C.)	1934
1927	
Miss Window	1949
1928	
Miss Foster	1935
Miss Reid	1930
Miss Hill (P.T.C.)	1929
also 1930 – 1932	
1929	
Miss Stockdale	1933
1930	
Miss McGuinness	1931
Miss Ward	1938
1931	
Miss Bourne	1933
Miss Traill	1932
1932	
Miss Wilkinson	1938
Miss Baldwin	1962
Miss Pugh	1962
1933	
Mrs Dyer	1945
(helped out several times plus part-time after 1945)	

	Year left
1933	
Miss Cope	1939
Miss Goodrich (P.T.C.)	1938
1934	
Miss White	1937
Miss Fowler	1946
1935	
Miss Niven (P.T.C.)	1946
Miss Barnes	1939
Miss Gay	1939
Miss Rofe	1939
1936	
Miss Barton	1944
1938	
Miss Belcher	1941
Miss Lewis	1944
Miss De la Mare	1944
(1936 – 1938 P.T.C.)	
1939	
Miss Jones	1943
Miss M. E. Matkin (O.G.)	1940
Miss Tyrrell	1943
Miss Weinemanne	1944
1940	
Miss Woodger	
(Catering Staff 1934)	1971
Miss Baker	1941
Mlle Vigo	1942
1941	
Miss Dugon	1943
Miss Grosset	1945
Miss Kett	1947
1942	
Mrs Anderson	1946
Miss Ablett	1943

	Year left
1942	
Miss Wood (seconded from Woodford County High School)	1943
1943	
Miss Mounsey-Wood	1945
Miss Ferguson	1949
Miss Sandy	1946
Miss Pengilly	1959
Miss Rooth	1955
Miss Tutt	1951
Miss Johnson	1944
1944	
Miss Reichsman	1949
Miss Neel	1950
Miss Wright	1947
Miss Burnell Carter	1964
1945	
Mrs Clutton-Brock	1947
Mrs Stuart-William	1949
Mrs Horn	1962
Miss Cull	1948
Miss Dodd	1948
1946	
Miss Wells (O.G.)	1973
Miss Hunt	1947
Mr Freyhan	1949
Mrs Anderson	1947
Miss Llewelyn	1947
Miss Sas	1972
1947	
Mrs Fry (part-time and temporary periods)	1949
Miss Todman	1982
Miss Broadway	1975
Mrs Gray also 1959 – 1968	1952
Miss Helliwell	1963
Miss Jackson	1972
Miss Spice	1949

	Year left
1947	
Miss Ware	1952
Miss Flood also 1949 – 1956	1948
Mr Lee	1949
Miss Stonebridge	1961
1948	
Mrs Walker	1963
Miss Thomas	1950
Miss Arnot	1964
1949	
Miss McBride	1949
Miss MacIver	1949
Miss Nadin	1954
Miss Holmes	1953
Miss Key	1974
Mrs Childs	
Miss Warne	1952
Miss Carr	1956
Mrs Wood also 1975 and 1978 –	1952
Miss Pace	1954
Mrs Tanner	1950
1950	
Miss Höcker	1969
Miss J. Davies	1952
Miss Dixon	1952
Mrs Prouse	1952
1951	
Miss Whysall	1952
Miss Neave	1955
Miss Hills	1953
1952	
Mrs Fernie	1954
Miss F. R. Davies	1956
Miss Davison	1956
Miss Dudley	1955
Miss Hanson	1955
Miss Kennelly	1954
Miss Tonner	1959

	Year left
1953	
Miss Ibbotson	1955
Miss Southwell	1978
Miss Norwood	1959
1954	
Mrs Saunders	1971
Mrs Phillipson	1957
Mlle Espelet	1955
Mrs Bryan	1956
Miss Flarty	1963
Miss Walter	1961
1955	
Miss Cobb	1956
Miss Jacobi	1957
Miss Searancke	?
Mrs Britton (O.G.)	1958
also 1962 –	1982
Miss Dixon	1956
Miss Young	1956
Mrs Deveson	1956
1956	
Miss Austin	1958
Miss Taylor	1959
Miss French	1963
Miss Whitehead	1960
Miss Houghton	1958
Mrs Dunstan	?
also 1962 –	1963
Mrs Major	1957
Miss Robinson	1969
Mrs Jones	1965
1957	
Miss Fossey	1963
Miss Richardson	1959
Mrs Booth (part-time)	1959
Miss Askwith (part-time)	?
Mrs Dawson (part-time)	?
Miss Birtwhistle	1970
Mrs Black (part-time)	?
Miss Freeman (part-time)	?
Mrs Richards (part-time	?
Miss Waller	1963

	Year left
1957	
Miss Warner	1957
Mrs Boyson	1963
1958	
Miss Gilroy	1975
Mrs Lines	1970
Miss Smith (Mrs Hudson)	1962
Miss Willis (Mrs Hartley)	1963
Miss Myers	1960
Miss Moss	1960
1959	
Miss W. E. Dickson	
Miss Elliott	1968
Miss Jenkins	1962
Miss Kingham (Mrs Buss) (O.G.)	1966
also 1976 – 1977	
Miss Lewis	1962
Miss Millar	1961
1960	
Mrs Andrews	1961
Miss Freestone	1961
Miss Hamblin	1961
Mrs James	1964
Miss Palmer	1966
1961	
Mrs Thompson	1966
Miss Evans	1963
Miss Grigg	1981
Miss Peters	1970
Miss Southcott	1964
Mrs M. Taylor	1963
Mrs Wardell	1963
Mrs A. Hughes	1972
Mrs Blayney	?1965–?1966
1962	
Mrs Cottrell	1964
Miss Green (Mrs Ross)	1966
Miss Holmes (Mrs Wright)	1965

	Year left
1962	
Miss G. Smith	1964
Miss M. H. Smith	1973
Miss Wachsmann	1963
Miss E. M. Davies	1965
Mrs Gore	1965
Mrs Stokes	1965
1963	
Mrs S. Smith	1966
also 1977 –	
Miss Eldergill (Mrs Bennett)	1967
Miss Allison	
Miss Blake	1978
Miss Burrows	1965
Miss Clark	1965
Miss Dickinson	1967
Mrs Edmondson	1966
Miss Goucher	1965
Miss Hatton	
Miss Theaker	1967
Miss Williment (Mrs Barnes)	1969
1964	
Miss Burchell	1969
Miss Greasley	1977
Miss Grenier	1964
Miss Hopkinson	1974
Mrs Taylor	1968
Miss Titchner	1967
1965	
Miss Jones (Mrs Perry) (O.G.)	1968
also 1982 –	
Miss Durham	
Miss Bignell	1967
Mrs Gröger	
Mrs Heard	1966
Miss Hurn (Mrs Bowles)	1968
Mrs Nicholls	1981
Mrs Rogers	1975
Miss Talbot	1966

	Year left
1966	
Miss East	1966
Miss Allen	1969
Miss Brundell	1974
Miss Clarke (Mrs Readings)	1970
Miss Glyn Evans	1968
Miss Grimwood	1968
Mrs Lowe	1969
also 1970 – 1971	
Miss McGaw (Mrs Barrell) (later part-time)	1972
Miss Stewart	1969
Mrs Wilkinson	1968
1967	
Miss Harris	1967
Miss Warner	1971
Mrs Casey	1968
Miss Scott (Mrs Williams)	1970
Miss Swann (Mrs Powell)	1972
Miss Thick	1972
Mr P. J. King	1969
also 1974 – 1975	
1968	
Mrs Southgate (Mrs Sutton)	1981
Miss Bain	1970
Miss Bird (Mrs Ramsey)	1971
Mrs Callaway	
Miss Cooper	1969
Miss Haycock	1972
Mrs Metherell	1970
Mrs Sampson	1972
also 1977 –	
Mrs Vellacott	1974
1969	
Mrs Harris	1970
Mrs Ballard	1972
Miss Cairns (Mrs Churcher)	
Mr Daycock	1971
Mrs Daycock	1971
Miss M. P. Jones	

	Year left
1969	
Miss Morgan	1972
Mrs Nelson	1972
Mrs Shaw	1970
Mrs J. P. Smith	
1970	
Miss Brown	1974
Miss Crocker	
Mrs Laird	
Miss Richards (as Mrs Barlow part-time and temporary periods 1977 onwards)	1975
Mrs Tovey	1973
Miss L'Angellier	1974
Mrs Proudfoot	
Miss Hannaford	1973
Mrs Richardson	
1971	
Mrs Sharrock	1973
Mrs Wibberley	1974
Mrs Barney	1973
Mrs Beard also 1982 –	1974
Mrs Bignell	1972
Miss Harris also as Mrs Rider 1979 –	1973
Mrs Haynes	1974
Mrs M. Hughes	1972
1972	
Miss Hoare	1975
Mrs Warren	1977
Miss Warren (Mrs Edwards)	1977
Mrs K. Wright	
Miss Andrews (Mrs Weatherby)	1980
Mrs Audsley	1974
Mrs Clifton	
Mrs Elliott	1974
Miss Gascoyne (Mrs Cook)	1975
Miss Geary (Mrs D. Jones)	1975

	Year left
1972	
Miss Rose	1975
Miss Shaw	1977
Mrs Toyn	
Mrs Vivian	1975
Mrs Wardell	1973
Miss Millard (Mrs P. Young)	1979
1973	
Mr Bull	1975
Mrs Griffiths	1974
Mrs Hutchinson	1974
Miss Bennett	
Mrs Burton	
Mrs Dixon	1975
Mrs How	
Mrs McKinnon	1975
Mrs Paradiso	1977
Mr Sanders	
Mr Stevens	1975
Mrs Watkin (also 1980 – 1981)	1977
Miss Wren	1979
1974	
Mrs Walters (née Nicholl) (O.G.) also 1977 –	1974
Miss Adams (Mrs Pattinson)	1977
Mrs Bitton	1978
Miss Clark (Mrs Larman)	
Miss Clowes (Mrs Winson)	
Mr Coombe	
Miss Evans	1976
Mrs Grattidge	
Mr Miller	
Mrs Scott	
Mr Weatherby	1980
Mrs Barnes	
Mrs Hall, (née Franklin) (O.G.)	1975
Rev. C. Hamel-Cooke	1978
Mrs Hutton	1977
Mrs Moss	1977

1974	Year left
Mrs Taylor	1981
Mrs Thomas, (née Bull) (O.G.)	1976

1975	
Mrs Gurr	1978
Mrs Turnbull	1978
Mrs Argent	1977
Miss Barnes	1979
Mrs Charlesworth	1978
Dr Eason	1980
Mrs Kelly	
Mrs Marquand	1976
Miss S. Wells	1979
Mrs Weldon	1978
Mrs Midgley	

1976	
Miss Byrom-Taylor	1977
Mrs Reid	1980
Mrs Wootton, (née Stone) (O.G.)	1977
Mrs Bennett	1977
Rev. D. Lewthwaite	1979
Mrs Roe	
Mrs Sylvester	1977

1977	
Mrs Corless	
Miss Davis (Mrs Baker)	1979
Miss Ibbott (Mrs Eason) (O.G.)	1982
Miss McGeoch	1979
Miss McLaren (Mrs A. Smith)	
Mrs Pearson	
Miss Ratcliffe (O.G.)	
Miss Talbot	
Mrs Weston, (née Griffin) (O.G.)	

1977	
Mrs Anderson	
Mrs Bunker	1980
Miss Angell (Mrs Scorer)	
Mrs Button	1979

1977	Year left
Mrs Harris	1979
Mrs Wheeler	1978
Mrs Maddison	

1978	
Miss Burnell	1981
Miss Bruce	
Miss Calvert	
Mrs Davies	
Mrs Hoggar	
Mrs J. Jones	
Mrs Kelley	
Mrs D. Wright	

1979	
Mrs Betts	
Miss Fisher	
Mr Webb	1980
Mrs M. Young	
Mrs Ellis	1980
Mrs Ireland	
Mrs Rogers	1981

1980	
Mrs Reast	
Mrs Banister	
Miss Benfield	
Mrs Chubb	
Mrs Lopez-Real	
Miss McFarland	
Miss Palmer	
Mrs J. Perry	
Mrs Stephenson	

1981	
Mrs Clark	
Mrs Mapes	
Mrs Daniels	
Mrs Reed	
Mlle Roulon	
Mrs Kapsalis	

1982	
Miss K. Dickson	
Mrs Grafton	

Notes:

S.T. = Student Teacher
O.G. = Old Girl
P.T.C. = Physical Training College. This was founded by Miss Stansfeld in 1903. Members of staff thus indicated were appointed and paid by the College. Miss Stansfeld herself does not appear in the O.G. Newsletters (1912 onwards) as a current member of staff, but her name remains on the salary lists in Miss Dolby's Log-book until 1922–23.

Since it has not always been easy to distinguish between part-time and full-time service, this distinction has ordinarily been omitted. Temporary (short-period) members of staff are not always recorded.

When the school opened there were in addition to the Headmistress 4 full-time and 2 part-time members of staff: in 1982 there are more than 50 full-time, and over 20 part-time members.

The pupil–staff ratios calculated from figures given in H.M.I. Reports are as follows:

1906	19.4:1	1932	15:1
1913	15.7:1	1949	21.3:1
1923	19:1	1956	18.3:1

The present (1982) ratio is 15.5:1

ANNUAL TUITION FEES AT THE FOUR SCHOOLS

	1903	1910	1920	1930	1940	1950	1960	1970	1980
BEDFORD	13	16	22	30	32	68	144	297	1,500
HIGH	15	16	17	24	25	72	126	249	1,158
MODERN	4	5	7	12	15	30	54	153*	1,098
DAME ALICE	5	5	6	10	10	24	51	144*	933

NOTE: Upper School Tuition Fees to the nearest £1.

*These figures partly dictated by cut in Capitation Grant of £30 in 1968.

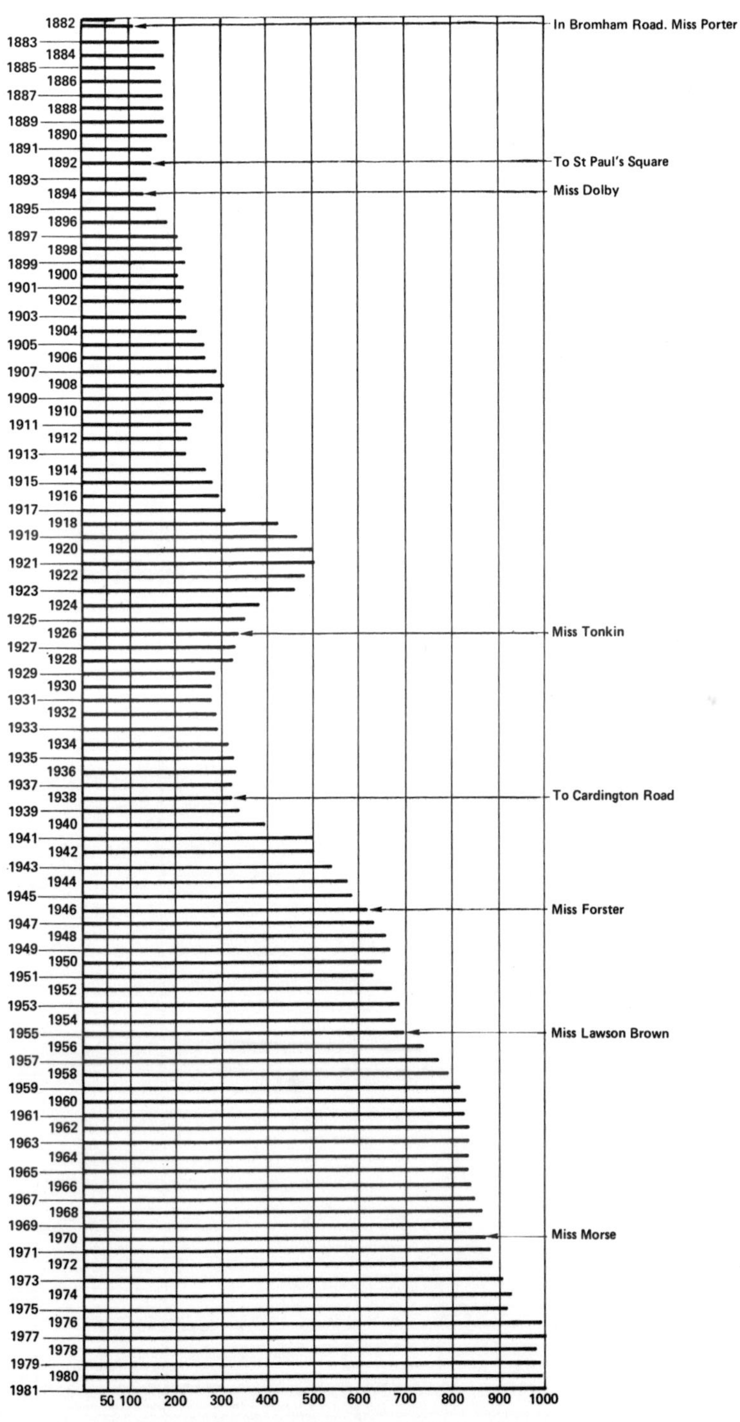

NUMBER OF PUPILS IN SCHOOL 1882-1981